"The best triggers for *would-be* sages."
- **LA Weekly**

"Sharp, profuse and mind-boggling philosophical jab: a tall order but effortlessly administered." - **Philosophy Daily**

"Bozzino's unique storytelling style smoothly transports *philistines* into a realm of deep introspection and contemplation, providing a fresh outlook on timeless philosophical questions that have long fascinated humanity." - **Australian Times**

"A sleek holiday to discover humanities in the history, with a critical eye. Bozzino not only makes philosophy trendy and in tune with public skepticism, but also nurtures responsibility to go deeper, untangle, take a stand and solve what he points out, by skilfully employing argument tight turns, storyline steep slopes and mesmerising register inversions." - **The Washington Mail**

"*Philosophy Trips* is destined to become a cult classic, shaking world naives with soulful oratory and enlightened perspectives. It is a tour de force that showcases the immense talent and breadth of knowledge possessed by this young Renaissance man."
- **Les Temps Modernes**

"The book is very agile, on a crowd-awakening mission with enormous scope. The result is therefore a bird's eye view that addresses almost all disciplines in a discretionary way, without too much indulgence, as a pop philosophy compendium would. Still, Bozzino keeps it brutally thorough for the benefit of first-time speculators, each chapter is stuffed full of philosophical references and food for thought - for your emancipation." - **Book Life**

"The most encyclopaedic & easygoing guide, giving philosophy new blood and saving us weeks in the library or years in the cerebral abyss." - **Susan Orlean, Author of *1000 steps to Wisdom* and *Let the Grown-ups Play***

"Gifted storyteller, at his trade debut, feeds the curious with high-intensity, critical training and strokes of imagination." - **The Telegraph India**

# PHILOSOPHY TRIPS

# PHILOSOPHY TRIPS

*A Naive's Guide*

VINCENT BOZZINO

Libertine Press

## AUTHOR'S NOTE

This is a series of university papers I originally wrote between 2018 and 2022 for my BA course in Philosophy at University of London.
My outlook was seldom well-received by examiners:
I am proud of that.

The information in this book was correct at the time of publication, but the Author does not assume any liability for loss or damage caused by errors or omissions.

© 2024 by Vincent Bozzino

Libertine Press
34 Berkley Square
London, UK W1J5BF

www.libertinepress.com

All rights reserved. No part of this book may be reproduced or used in any manner without written permission by Vincent Bozzino, except in the case of study or brief quotations embodied in social media, critical articles and reviews. This includes re-printing, distributing and retailing without consent.

First published, 2024

Paperback ISBN 978-1-7392377-3-8
Ebook ISBN 978-1-7392377-4-5

A catalogue record for this title is available from the British Library, the Library of Congress and the Senate House Library.

# CONTENTS

*Author's Notes*

**INTRODUCTION**   1

    I   History of Philosophy   5

    II   Knowledge   11

    III   Logic   33

    IV   Morality   53

    V   Ethics   69

    VI   Mind   85

    VII   Metaphysics   101

    VIII   Science   113

    IX   Language   131

    X   Aesthetics   148

    XI   Religion   166

    XII   Politics   196

References and Bibliography   222

**RECOMMENDED READING LIST**   231

*To Nietzsche
and Co.
for
changing my life*

# Introduction

Philosophy is the mother of all other disciplines, because throughout the history, it gave birth to every other discipline.

The relationship between philosophy and all other subjects equals the bond between a mother, and her children: it continues to play a pivotal role by leading the offsprings, with discretion and no credit.

My journey, just like any philosopher's, started alone in curious wondering and hopefully will be crowded at the output.

There is power in the act of pausing life and question around. Searching for truth is addictive, especially when that is, in fact, only a human, fragile longing for beauty behind all.

Philosophical inquiry is puzzling and deserting, a labyrinth with no way out yet a splendid, life-long adventure of an individual striving for beauty - for better - whose eye-opening beginning, then goes up and up to never end. After all, true education is not the learning of facts; it's rather the training of the mind to think.

So what is education without philosophy? Get ready to leave your naivety. **Fasten your seat belt**.

I cannot wait for you to join us selected few, deep down inside, high up above and try your luck too at becoming *superhuman*.

"The unexamined life is not worth living"
**Socrates**

# CHAPTER I

# History of Philosophy

## *Philosophy of History*

A fascinating quote, frequently attributed to Thucydides - and one of my favourite - goes "history is philosophy teaching by example".

Forcefully, R.G. Collingwood insisted on how "all history is, in fact, the history of thought".

One traditional view of our history, now discarded, is that it is virtually synonymous with the history of ideas: history is composed of human actions, human actions have to be explained by intentions, and intentions cannot be formed without ideas.

Our past is characterised by armed conflicts of powerful states, worldwide explorations, cultural movements or social transformations, each ultimately seeking to achieve *ideals* - a proposed standard of perfection, beauty or excellence in life. As a result, one shall be persuaded enough to endorse that history is, symbolically, the documentation of human thought and of intellectuals, people who conceptualize, discuss, express about and practically (or philosophically) concern themselves with their time being on Earth.

At its core, history is driven by a generative search for a "true discourse of the past". This dialectical emphasis on the human aspect has made people the central subject of narratives in the classic discourses of modern history; as a result, history has taken on a philosophical sense that is broader than just an actual narrative of the human past.

History often emblematizes the production of events with transformative potentials that lead into the future: this is like a temporal pattern, highlighted by the *signifier* of history, which connects the past, present and future.

Historical temporality is therefore rooted in the idea that autonomous human subjects are endowed with historical subjectivity.

In other words, historical truth can be considered an effect of the historiographical production method. History can be said to be nothing but a philosophy, an allegory itself.

**Allegory of History**
Nikolaos Gysis, 1892

For instance, the foundation for professional historiography in East Asia was established by the court historian, author of the *Records of the Grand Historian*, also known by its Chinese name *Shiji*.

Throughout the Middle Ages and the Renaissance, history was often studied from a sacred or religious perspective. Around 1800, German philosopher and historian Georg Wilhelm Friedrich Hegel introduced philosophy and a more secular approach to historical study.

Hegel contended that universal history is the theater of the world, where the universal spirit (Weiltgeist) is made real, represented by states, peoples and individuals. Historical events always have a rationale, that is, all the events that have characterized the entire history of humankind necessarily had to happen.

The teleological philosopher is aware that in the eyes of the ordinary people, the events of history may be nothing more than a sequence of facts, disconnected from each other, without any precise logical character and without any purpose; for Hegel, nonetheless, historical progress of the world or "the becoming of history" bears precise logic and reason, attributable to the supreme divine will.

Such revolutionary conception would systematically influence and amaze posterity. One above all, Karl Marx's historical materialism intended as a process of overcoming human alienation in life and whose most cognate quote read:

> "History always repeats itself twice: the first time as a tragedy, the second as a farce."

Philosophy of history now reflects on the possible meaning of human history and constantly hypothesizes a teleological purpose (or finality) to its development: whether there is a design, function, goal or guiding principle in the process of world history or not.

Ergo, the preferred method of historical study is *periodization*: focusing on events and progress that occur in eras, a beginning and an end can be defined for - at least, in principle.

Periodizations are used to think about the past in schematic terms: if this is a necessity in educational environments, though, these divisions have the defect of not being unambiguously accepted, let alone definitive.

The different answers given to evolution and philosophical problems can be usefully examined by following the philosophical development of history (or the historical development of philosophy): where there is a close correspondence between the conception and representation of historical reality, and those critical perspectives of reality, crisply express the characteristic features of an epoch.

As a matter of fact, there are general accounts with indefinable and often overlapping contours between philosophy and history, for instance, attempts to investigate the nature of history in relation to the free action of human beings.

> Opposed to the standard *historicist* type, philosophical theories of history include:
>
> - **history as a *regression***: the Greeks knew the myth of the Golden Age, described for example by Plato, an era of perfection humanity gradually declined from; an ideology reaffirmed by esoteric thinkers such as René Guénon, who identify modernity with the Dark Age of Kali Yuga, albeit with a view back to the origins;
> - **history as a cycle**: the ancient Stoics interpreted the world as a repetition of cosmic rounds, a vision taken up by Nietzsche with the myth of the eternal return and, in a different sense, by Spengler, who asseverated that civilizations are born, grow and die in a *necessary* way;
> - **history as a coincidence**: in particular, Schopenhauer pessimistically deems history aimless and purposeless - an imaginary and painful theater of mostly similar events. An anti-historicist attitude cut from the same cloth characterizes the thought of Karl Popper, skeptical of any teleology of becoming, tie-up with the structuralist and post-modern movement.

In the preface to his book entitled *Kitāb al-ʿibar* (The Book of Examples), the *Muqaddima*, Ibn Khaldūn (Tunis, 1332 - Cairo, 1406), stressed the seven errors that he believed all historians committed regularly.

In his critique, the Maghrebi historian and sociologist approached the past as mysterious and requiring interpretation - a *graphìa* of history. The originality of Ibn Khaldun was to affirm that the cultural difference of a period, other than its own does regulate the assessment of the relevant historical material, thus discriminating the criteria it would be possible to seek the review by.

The Arab scholar acknowledged how the analysis of a culture of the past implies experience, in addition to rational criteria, that is the study of history, especially its narrative is a test of critical examination or seed for historian's judgment.

The extent to which historians are influenced in the writing of history by their own groups and loyalties - in primis, their nation-state - still feeds the Gordian knot.

Khaldūn championed critical thinking and fathered historiography, the supervisory study of the methods and foundations of history, with an academic focus on the authority of the stories, rather than the credibility of the transmitter. Philosophy of history sits above and has levers of diagnostic control on either discipline, in the typical fashion of all the philosophical branches.

In the 20th century, several other methods of historical study have been proposed: some historians research universal history, others focus their work on specific practices (i.e. chronology, demography, historiography, genealogy, palaeography or cliometrics) or certain areas (e.g. the history of Brazil, the history of China or the history of science).

In recent years, postmodernists have questioned the validity and necessity of the study of history, claiming that all record is based on personal interpretation of sources.

Philology and philosophy are also closely paired by history, just like they allegedly appear in Botticelli's *Primavera*, according to a recent artistic interpretation of the famous work.

Considerations on human history or the philosophy of history, by reflex, revive the historical relationship between philology and philosophy (philology as the origins of humanities), and disclose the philological aspect of history - the shared *"love for the word"* with philosophy.

With wide humanistic overlap, eros is addressed both in the philological and philosophical enterprise, respectively **(1)** for the ancient semantics and the *episteme* of a word, as *logos, mythos* of an idea to be investigated archeologically and **(2)** for the idea itself, as *ontos, ethos* in its historical development to be transformed dialectically, driven by the human urgency of a philosophical detachment from the *doxa*.

In one of his genealogical studies, Michel Foucault simply referred to "Words and Things" (philology and philosophy) but the relation between those two is not yet given once and for all. For instance, philosophy is widely cursed with problematic fragmentation that fails to unite the great branches of thought (humanistic and scientific), while philology remains a lost art, with an uncertain place in intellectual history.

Luckily, history is a human science and human beings can never stop the quest for a sense to history, because its study has a projection toward the future as a benchmark for social change.

> "History conceals everything, yet everything reveals"
> **POPE JOHN PAUL II**

To date, history appears to constitute a subject for reflection that is as interesting for philosophy as other inquiry forms.

We cannot dispute the historical dimension of philosophy as a human activity, not entirely indifferent to each philosopher's historical sentiment. The wise conclusion is that every philosopher is a child of their time and their thought should never be actualised, only applied.

# CHAPTER II

# Knowledge

*Epistemic Findings*

---

What distinguishes knowledge from mere belief?
How do we acquire knowledge?

---

*What do you know and how do you know it?* Everybody hints at these big questions, at least once, in a conversation. As humans, we compulsively doubt and naturally seek for evidence to beliefs, experience to truth and reasonableness to confusion.

We're all interested in the world we live in, to a certain extent, and how do we make sense of it, while living. In sophisticated terms, how do we acquire the reality therein, at any one time, the totality that exists and constitutes the "outside" of our individuation?

When we truly begin to ponder on this, a precursory interrogation arises: how do we know, what we know? And in the matter of how do we acquire knowledge about everything we know: what makes knowledge? What is a belief in something?

Epistemology is the philosophical study concerned with those questions.

A belief is the attitude of someone who recognizes *p* as true, admitting its validity on the level of objective truth, in the sense that believing *p* is equivalent to affirming *p* is true, or at least that there are sufficient reasons to prove that. According to this acceptation, a difference in meaning leaps up between the notion of *certainty* and that of *doubt*.

The concept of certainty, in the history of philosophy, fuses with that of truth to specify the property of what exists in an absolute sense (ἀλήθεια, alétheia) and cannot be false.

Epistemology particularly invests us, for the value derived from its subject matter. The intrinsic value of knowledge lies in the fact that we can see reality as it is, regardless of our interests and preconceptions. Hence, we worry in possessing truth (through knowledge) rather than mere belief.

What accounts for "knowledge" is a debate, as old as philosophy itself. The theory of knowledge is essentially concerned with delineating the boundary between justified belief and "doxa" (opinion).

The main problem of epistemology is to understand precisely what we need, in order to know. In broad terms, the pitfalls are communication, meaning, thought reference and social dynamics, which altogether create an agency problem inherent in knowledge production and transmission.

A widespread definition of knowledge wants it as a "theory of justification" of the truth of beliefs, also known as tripartite analysis (for knowing is analyzed into three components). Justification is the reason why we all have beliefs. In case of doubt, justification will reduce or remove uncertainty.

Consequently, knowledge can be summarized as *"justified true belief"*, any case constituted by belief and always of truth, and reality:

- *p*
- *a* believes that *p*,
- *a*'s belief is justified.

The standard account of knowledge, which derives from the Platonic dialogue *Theaetetus*, puts in the foreground the importance of the necessary - even if not sufficient - conditions, so that an affirmation may pertain to knowledge. Still, this is not always the case.

When one defines knowledge as *"justified true belief"* (abb. JTB), then one may easily glimpse situations where we know something without knowing that we know; if one believes $p$ to be true, has a justification to believe $p$ and $p$ is accurate, it might still be the case that one does not have knowledge that the justification is good but that $p$ is, in fact, true.

The foregoing famous challenge to the sufficiency of the tripartite analysis is the *Gettier problem*. In his 1963 paper, *"Is Justified True Belief Knowledge?"*, Edmund Gettier demonstrated with two counter-examples, that there are cases whereby individuals can have a justified, true belief, yet still fail to know; for the reasons of the idea while justified, turn out to be false.

The purpose is to show how the conditions imposed by the definition of propositional knowledge, in the customary standard within the epistemological dispute, are necessary but not sufficient requirements to be able to verify that a subject S knows a proposition $p$, and that the definition is therefore incomplete.

**The School of Athens (1509–1511) by Raphael** depicts famous classical Greek philosophers in an idealized setting, inspired by ancient Greek architecture

Corrective theories have been presented, in an attempt to integrate the definition of knowledge with further conditions, or to clarify the stipulation more precisely.

The most obvious responses to Gettier's challenge cross-examined the "justification" of any justified true belief; what might be called a "JTB+G" analysis, formulated upon the addition of some fourth prerequisite — a *"no Gettier prob-*

*lem"* condition — to rules of justification, truth, and belief, so as to form a set of necessary and jointly sufficient conditions.

Throughout the history of philosophy, the subject of justification has played a significant role in the value of knowledge.

Pressured to operate a *true-false* choice or judge whether an action is appreciable or reprehensible, philosophers resorted to an authority with characteristics such that its evaluation is definitive and justifying. In the absence of that authority, any claim would be rejected.

Whilst on the one side there never was an urge to justify whatsoever belief, for the possibility itself of belief - and knowledge - is denied regardless (skepticism), on the other there has been an obsessive research for an indisputable candidate X, the justification of any belief is said to be contingent upon (evidentialism).

The ways we come to know, or the justifiers we employ, circumvent extensive literature as plausible evidence to any justified belief. Generally speaking, these may be divided in two main blocks: experience and reason.

At this junction, the topic of justification is not only of the essence to convene the most accurate definition of knowledge, but what is more extremely valuable for a clearer insight into the world, as a whole, the nature of being and their relationship as well as concepts in the middle.

Evidentialism, the strongest attitude for gnoseological justification, expresses an undeniable fact: the nature of reality, in general, exists independently of the knowing subject as its opponent therein (realism).

In doing so, justification may use exclusively the evidence of the senses, such as perception or an authoritative testimony, leading to knowledge *a posteriori* (empiricism) or vice versa, employ reason as the only source of knowledge about the world *a priori* (rationalism).

For its evaluative judgment, justification is often associated with rationality: to clarify, much like it is intuitive to say that a justified belief is a rational belief, it is equally intuitive to say that somebody is reasonable, when they have justified belief.

Since Aristotle, the process of reasoning has been labelled based on its form.

> **Deductive reasoning**, by intellect or logical deduction, on the basis of deductive inference (through an outward process, from universal to particular); what shall be defined as a way to knowledge "by analysis".
>
> **Inductive reasoning**, by intuition, as a result of inductive inference (*epagoghé*, from particular to universal); what shall be regarded as a way to knowledge "within".

Noteworthy, the inevitable degeneration of rationalism and its train of thought presumes the supremacy of reality over concepts (also known as *universals*), the object over the subject and therefore, a blind trust in the ability of reason to produce on its own, knowledge (dogmatism).

Testimony is a peculiar way of spreading knowledge and intrinsically subsists on someone else, feeding off the experience vicariously.

The recognition of other minds and the correlation of the state of joint evidence, between cognitive subjects, grants the inclusion of testimony in the realm of experience.

An analogous subset, memory also entails experience, albeit reminiscent from the past, as a way to knowledge by remembering.

Externalism claims that factors deemed "external" can be conditions of epistemic justification, for a belief, to count as knowledge.

For instance, I may not know that I am writing on a paper with a pen, just now but as I can identify the surroundings and immediately relate to facts that are entirely external to myself, the state of the external world justifies my belief - I know I am writing now.

Using logical notation:

$$(\forall x) \{B(x) \rightarrow [K(x) \leftrightarrow JE(x)]\}$$
any justified belief is knowledge, if and only if, it is justified externally.

A popular form of externalism is reliabilism, whereby rather than justification, all that is required is that the belief be the product of a reliable process: something that has caused the subject to have that belief.

Notwithstanding, a unique consequence of reliabilism (and other forms of externalism) is that I could have a justified belief that I am working at the desk, without knowing I am justified.

Powerfully, it is yet undetermined which cognitive processes are "reliable", thus should we adopt reliabilism, we also ought to concede that "we do not always know, whether some of our beliefs are justified" (even though there is a *fact of the matter*).

There are further externalist alternatives instigated, including Robert Nozick's arguments for a requirement that knowledge *"tracks the truth"*, more eloquently, knowledge as a true belief that tracks the relevant fact in a reliable way (adaequatio rei et intellectus).

Tracking theories seem to contain difficulties of their own, pointing to Descartes, who first suggested we shall not consider the concept of knowledge infallible, for basically we possess error-prone senses, which may deceive us as we perceive (or engage with) the external world.

And in response, we ought not to consider any of the truth-tracking conditions "through a defect, flaw or failure" as knowledge. Such rendition crumbles unconvincing, because someone's belief tracks justified knowledge, yet not truth and the possibility of "true knowledge" begs the question.

Metaphysics alone triggers gobs of epistemological implications, in cases where evidentialism - intended as material - is impossible, like Popper's philosophy of falsificationism reminds. Further, the truth-tracking account errs in and then seeks to find the simplest conclusion (abductive reasoning).

Conversely, in the light of rationalism, internalism defends that all knowledge-yielding conditions are within the psychological purview of those who gain knowledge.

In the teeth of the evidence, the justification for a belief is internal to the believer in two main ways, at times overlapping: the believer becoming aware, by reflective access to the justifier (access internalism) or the believer's mind alone, establishing the epistemic justifier (ontological internalism).

Upon the line of reasoning, many philosophers argue that there may be self-evident ideas that do not need to be demonstrated, at all and on which, therefore, all other beliefs may be legitimately based (foundationalism).

A remarkable, historical example of foundationalism is traceable in the Cartesian argument that, at the end of the *Discourse on the Method*, comes to the conclusion that there is a clear and distinct, evident truth, which can be taken as the pillar of all other knowledge - the set of beliefs culminates in special, justified beliefs called "basic beliefs" as properly incorrigible.

The most distinguishing rival of the foundationalist theory of justification contradicts that a belief, in order to be justified must belong to a coherent belief system (coherentism).

As epistemological theory, coherentism is branded as too permissive; for instance, saying "I am a butterfly" - a false proposition - is however consistent with the group of propositions that follows: "Before I was a caterpillar", "I can fly", etc.

In both of Gettier's actual examples, the justified true belief came about as the result of entailment (Case I) and secondly, its coherent application to a "putative" belief (Case II). Since Gettier, knowledge is no longer widely conceived at the mercy of a justification requirement only.

Foundationalism and coherentism, as conventional theories of justification, hold an infinite regress not to be a valid one. On the contrary, infinitism still counts the latter, as a positive resolution to the epistemological problem of justification, whensoever the infinite series of relations, a belief derives its justification from, continues endlessly or without a circular argument.

In the analysis of the phenomena, the existence and behaviour of the single and the outside world consistently counterpose each other.

On the whole, then, we observe the possibility of knowledge to develop in the epistemic form, halfway between rationalism and empiricism, wherein elements derived from experience and others that do not refer to empirical data, coexist.

In other words, reason plays a highly active role in the process of knowledge, but cannot exclude sensitive experience, therefore knowledge generates by way of judgment, in a critical synthesis of mental and physical (criticism).

Criticism was a watershed in the history of humankind, mapping out for the first time during the Enlightenment, the origin of our epistemic findings and creating harmony between belief and justification (theory and action), with the tenet that human reason is simultaneously judge and defendant, in the acquisition (and transmission) of knowledge.

Congeries of new and old epistemological theories compete for attention but accepted paradigms are still being routinely called into question by critical philosophy, which had a long-running domino effect on society.

Easily identifiable cases of critical approaches are Marxism, behavioural economics, psychoanalysis, postmodernism, gender studies and feminism.

So far, the path presented above illustrates how the problem of reality, genealogically springs from an epistemological one: the possibility of an "objective" knowledge and an ascertained difference between the object ("ob-iectum" = "standing in front") from the knowing subject ("sub-iectum" = "standing under").

A fortiori, we could not doubt for a moment the presence of the object, as of minor importance to that of the individual, the subject being. Nonetheless, the intricacies of the latter paved the way for backstage epistemological tittle-tattle, fuelling a meta-ontological row.

At the heart of the idle talk, a very plausible attack to reality, with respect to the philosophical tradition of realism: idealism. This vantage point is best represented as the offspring of nominalism, a long-standing doctrine that denies ontological consistency to the cognitive principles of the intellect.

Ergo, in idealist districts, the phenomenon of reality is denied in the role of ontologically autonomous, rather materiality is nothing but the reflection of an activity internal to the subject.

This perspective has analogies with philosophical constructivism, a consequent position selling that it does not make sense to pursue an objective representation of reality, for the world of our experience - the world we live in - is the result of our recreation.

In pursuing a constructivist line of action, though, we are also propelled to the all-dangerous opportunity of choosing faith - or what is broadly called *irrationality* - above reason, chained on our own lens and self-serving perceptions (fideism).

Presuppositional justification may be classified as more closely allied to [logically invalid] foundationalism and coherentism, for taking the truth of implicit, first principles and the non-truth of *entailment*, for granted, in the theoretical frame of reference.

The impact of Kant and the fervent criticism stood the test of bavardage, shifting the light on the epistemic interaction between subject and object; a pivotal element for the development of an actual study and organization of phenomena that manifest through experience, in time and space (phenomenology).

With critical knowledge through judgment, the subject attracted all philosophical attention, at the expense of external physical reality, whose existential value is put, so to speak, "in brackets".

Phenomenology sanctioned, *de facto*, the epistemic rapport, whereby the subject confronted intentionally an object, regardless of the real existence of the latter (transcendental phenomenology).

Out of all these, the principle behind Gettier's examples was that the justification for the belief is flawed or incorrect, but the belief turns out to be true *by sheer luck*.

Early critics inferred that the definition of knowledge should be easily conformed, so that knowledge is justified true belief that does not depend on *false premises*.

Richard Kirkham has notably argued that the only definition of knowledge that could ever be immune to all counterexamples is infallibilism, understood as evidence or justification providing a belief, with such strong grounds that it must be true and perhaps cannot be rationally doubted.

To qualify as an item of knowledge, goes the theory, a belief must not only be true and justified, the justification of the belief must "necessitate" its truth (Richard L. Kirkham, 1984).

Amusing with logic symbols:

$$(\forall x) \{B(x) \rightarrow [K(x) \leftrightarrow JI(x)]\}$$
any justified Belief is Knowledge, if and only if, the Justification is Infallible.

Another feasible candidate for the fourth condition of knowledge is indefeasibility. On this account, knowledge is *undefeated* justified true belief — which is to say that a justified true belief counts as knowledge, iff there are no overriding or defeating truths, for the reasons that justify my belief.

By Cartesian lights, the cogito - *ergo sum et scribo* - the fact that I am here, *hic et nunc*, comfortable on a chair, writing [in more existential contexts, *mein das-in-der-Welt-sein* (my being-in-the-worldness)] - purports to form an indefeasible foundation of knowledge, for my belief that I am indeed, writing this book.

But according to defeasibility laws, it's a true proposition that does the defeating, not a believed proposition.

All in all, when we define "knowledge" in the canonical form of "justified true belief", we shan't forget that not everyone who knows that *p*, knows that they have a justified true belief that *p*. In other words, knowing does not imply knowing that one knows.

Over and over again, epistemology fights to show that knowledge is always fallible. How can that position be satisfying at all? It seems to many that we are eternally condemned to hope we are going in the right direction and that our beliefs about the external world are true.

Can't there be a compromise? Is there a way of tracking the truth with certainty? There is, generally speaking: by assuming that human intuition causes people to believe only such things that have not been proven to be false; and contrarily, to disbelieve whichever has not been proven to be true (tacit knowledge).

No matter how you label it, what intuition is, it is the ability to "know" something without knowing how we know it.

In summary, there is a case whereby if I know that $p$, I also know that I know that $p$, and such case, a graduate would style, is only where the belief is *second-countable*.

Usually, one may refute to regard intuition, as the only means of justification, for any belief, since relying just on *a priori* plainly breaches the necessary and sufficient conditions of knowledge; in fact, this produces a *first-countable belief*, i.e. a raw belief (prima facie).

Hence, experience is necessary - the impact with *a posteriori* - for the belief to designate itself with epistemic justification.

Since epistemic findings are not always valid, for the justified belief to qualify as knowledge, the justified belief must [equally] correspond and necessitate the truth, in that the belief justification is true and indubitable (infallibilism), and under any circumstances, overriding or defeating truths may not transform the same (indefeasibility).

Only then may we grant the justified belief the status of knowledge, if and only if, the belief is - what I like to call - a second-countable belief (ultima facie), that is to say a belief ascertainable, not just intuitively - *first-countable* - but also infallible and undefeated.

In formal reference,

$$(\forall x) \{B(x) \to [K(x) \leftrightarrow I(x) \wedge I(x)]\}$$
any justified Belief is Knowledge, if and only if, the Justification is Infallible, and Indefeasible.

Yet, knowing we *know something* is a process fraught with complications that any logical formula, as the ones accounted, perhaps, exclude.

**22 - VINCENT BOZZINO**

# The Possibility of Knowledge

How far can we go in understanding the world?

When we search for more evidence but we don't find it, philosophical practice triggers a knee-jerk reaction.

Essentially, what you know you're justified in believing, but there are exceptions. Typical case, I believe I know a lot about my surroundings, just now, perceptually.

I can reckon how I came here and I hope I remember times way afore that. I believe, I know something about the future. Immediately, I am going to gaze through the window, at the world outside and so forth.

*A brain in a vat that believes it is walking*

But how can I ascertain this is not just a vivid dream, as being the dream - all in all - a reality enhancer?

Isn't life itself, just a dream, not possessing any clear and distinct element, which allows to determine the difference between dream and reality?

Connotations of this kind are typical of skepticism, a pivotal philosophical position, in the context of epistemology, which denies the possibility of reaching - with knowledge - truth in an absolute sense.

Skepticism coloured the whole history of philosophy (and humanity) with impetus and essentially defines sciences, as knowledge is - at any moment - product of doubt.

Disbelief and suspicion express a typical stance of human beings, the perennial dissatisfaction with the amount of knowledge we can acquire or transmit.

The skeptic is therefore either the one who denies the possibility of knowing the truth (acatalepsy), for instance about what differs between dream and reality or the one who suspended the judgment, pending better information on which to deliberate (*epochè*), for instance in the enquiry of our own existence.

The pendulum of philosophical thought periodically swings between dogmatic affirmation and skeptical reaction. Dreaming provides a springboard for those who question, whether our own reality may be an illusion, in the first place.

When reality is indistinguishable from the dream (dream argument), consequently, they say I could only feed on simulated reality, deceived by a machine or a cunning, evil demon (the *"brain in a vat"* hypothesis).

What ultimately holds the skeptical choice are errors, our knowledge is always exposed to. Descartes is the first to chew over the fallacy of the senses and the lawfulness of doubt, even in the face of mathematical judgments - the very existence of an external world.

Refusing to accept as true knowledge, anything that could be doubted, the French philosopher supposed that existence (the skeptical topic, par excellence) is the only thing, undoubtedly certain.

The form of existing does not require physical mass. Existence can be energy, interface between two forces; presence of a force (e.g. our hands) is a validation of existence (that is, I have hands). Awareness best defines existence. Scilicet, being aware is to exist, in some way.

The fact I am writing these words is evidence I am cogent and not dreaming. Ergo, the concept of cogency becomes one of awareness.

While Descartes strove to recast Platonic innatism into an autonomous gnoseological apparatus enabling reason to self-deduce the *"true"* a priori, skepticism bestowed modern philosophy an anti-doctrinaire horizon with thought forms that originally theorized the vanity of all knowledge (Māyā).

The numbing philosophy of Pyrrho (Pyrrhonism) taught that an absolute truth is achievable, albeit incommunicable: a theoretical and practical detachment is therefore, the best attitude, in front of things.

Ancient Greek schools of philosophical skepticism promoted a self-limited and pragmatic epistemological thesis, leading existence to the emotions of the contingency in an imperturbable and indifferent way.

Philosophical doubt does not imply, *per se*, the denial of the existence of the real world, rather that the theories about it cannot claim to explain deep nature.

Whenever skeptics shift to more radical positions, sponsoring that there is no principle of knowledge or truth (academic scepticism), the criteria for knowledge and justification intertwine wryly by identifying the end of doubt with what is evident, as first principle.

The knowledge generation or transmission causality dilemma stems from the following observation that all knowledge hatches from sources and all information sources are laid by knowledge - the problem of criterion is an ongoing issue aiming to discover the starting point of knowledge, what came first.

After a string of hyperbolic doubt (methodological scepticism), Descartes reached the conclusion that everything is built upon the basic knowledge that the self exists and that existence is exemplified in thought (*res cogitans*).

Upon this certainty, the speculator began to build a framework for unassailable scientific knowledge. Foundationalism argues that there are certain things that are absolutely known, at the core. Thus, one can analyze a phenomenon ("something"), by looking at whether that is dependent on anything else or not.

The methodical doubt differs from the skeptical doubt, which is instead a *"doubt to doubt"*, good for itself for the total distrust in the quality of humankind and the possibility of a true knowledge of reality.

Nonetheless, the Cartesian method continues to fudge the issue because, whereas "I think" is a recognizable truth, most of Descartes's subsequent metaphysical claims provide room for manoeuvre.

*"I think"* is only a subjective truth, where the person making the statement does so in reference to oneself; Kierkegaard fully grasped the concept of subjective truth and made it an integral part of his philosophical approach to all beliefs.

For some, knowing is an assent to truth, a belief of truth. Then, of course, there is the question *"what is truth?"*, and here we go again, investigating the epistemology.

Not being able to detail the extent of our knowledge and pinpoint the criterion of investigation follows that we are unable to justify any of our beliefs.

By this understanding, either we imply what constitutes knowledge and proceed to ascribe its limits (particularism) - eventually in a positivist key - or else we explicit that the possibility of knowledge, in primis, is questionable (methodism), receptive to skepticism, as in Descartes.

Skepticism is usually at risk of a drift in contradiction, especially as it always depends on an argument, *ab initio*; to resist the conclusion, the skeptic must always assume the knowledge, to whom the statement is made. An absolute and coherent skepticism, thus, is impossible, for it would be reduced to silence (*self-defeating argument*).

Contextualism was introduced, in part, to undermine skeptical arguments. The canon of contextualist epistemology is that knowledge attributions are context-sensitive; opposed to any general form of invariantism, which claims that knowledge is not context-sensitive (i.e. it is invariant).

For contextualists, when we attribute knowledge to somebody, the context within we use "knowledge claims", determines the standards by which "knowledge" is being attributed (or denied). Bear in mind, this is a semantic thesis about how *"knows"* works, rather than a full account of knowledge.

An proxy to contextualism, called contrastivism, uses semantic approaches to accost the problem of scepticism.

Instead of following the contextualist beat and insist that the meaning of ordinary *"knows"* can change with attributor context, contrastivists profess that the implicit "contrast clause" changes.

Plus, that the permissive, ternary structure (S knows that $p$ rather $q$) is sufficient to defeat skepticism.

It comes easy to ask, in ethical domains, whether it is on the cards to affirm that the truth is a relative issue or not. Alas, the appeal to context-sensitivity proves abortive.

With Kantian telescope, the critic individual, solicited to order their knowledge about the world, has recourse to "heuristics": shortcuts of judgment that consent to decide and lead to truth, even in the absence of sufficient data.

Contextualism about knowledge does not protect ordinary claims to know against skepticism, because its philosophical system undermines the relationship between the subject and the object, and its effects in the cognitive process - all the justifications are played down as contextual and all the fundamental, epistemic commitments do not admit any justification.

On a review of the whole literature, semantic theories - albeit interesting - are not as effective in epistemological industries, functioning as ultimate indicators of truth.

Everyone agrees that context is valuable in the quest for knowledge, thereby is aware of the epistemological significance of skepticism, as the midwife to bear truth.

On certainty, it seems that whatever one person may believe, another may disbelieve, while many others may be uncertain or even uninterested. Inevitably, the possibility of knowledge, the truth of reason and the truth of fact overlap in illuminating ways, notwithstanding fail to meet in context-sensitive conditions.

More radical types of skepticism subscribe to the principle that there is no certainty, at all. The idea expatiates on the possibility (or pluralism) of knowledge, in ordinary claims, in favour of a contextualist position, where fact is predicated upon context (thus, inevitably, on subject) rather than on evidence, thus mining the universalizability of truth.

Those who appeal to contextualism, in ordinary claims imply that all is relative, and therefore true reality does not exist. There is ultimately no authority, as a result, to decide whether an action is positive or negative, right or wrong (somewhat of a "situational ethics" in its maximum expression).

The denial of "universal truth" gives on to a natural logical contradiction, formal demonstrations can be provided for.

Any hypothetical "subjective" proposition (which is valid for a single, particular context), should it be true and demonstrated as such, would still have to fulfil the universality of its being true; that is, it must be true for each subject, in the context, such proposition is true for, only for a determinate, specific case.

Since figuring out truths is the central task of philosophy, many philosophers have struggled to put flesh on the bones of what can and cannot be known, or to create a formula to achieve undoubtable truths.

Philosopher of science Karl Popper found the loophole, arguing that a statement of truth has to be constructed in such a way as to be testable and, further, that there has to be a way to falsify the claim.

To circumscribe the horizon of truth, for many thinkers after him, meant defining veracity as instinct, emotions, correspondence between subject and object, consistency (logical or pragmatic) or even, as majority rule and *consensus gentium* (custom).

Ipso facto, knowledge becomes a belief from prudential justifications rather than epistemic ones, thus in necessity of being reconstructed as a *"sui generis"* cluster concept, rather than a single definition, like Timothy Williamson did.

In order for our beliefs to accurately depict the world, we ought desire and search only epistemically justified beliefs.

That possibility of knowledge is denied to us, the moment we let the notion of "truth" fit the anti-realist position, as "dependence on knowability", connecting our pre-philosophical intuitions with commons sense (subjectivism); simply put, when truth hails from what is not knowable in actuality, but rather by principle (or context).

In the exegetical dilemma of truth - highly influential on the concept of knowledge - the VR tech-driven, contemporary skepticism yet endorses that we do not know things, *per se*.

Perhaps, we see only what we can see, not all that is.

### DID YOU KNOW? ▼

Intelligence does not mean being clever. The word actually stands for "being able to read through", from the Latin *intus legere* (to read inside). Intelligent refers to an inquisitive, empathetic, intense or emotionally sensitive person. Like Einstein said: *"Any fool can know, the point is to understand"*.

According to Weaver, Rosenblum and Crossen, the news media is tainted truth: journalists fabricate crises to dramatize facts and government officials manipulate media to appear to be responding to crises, in a vicious circle of myth making and culture of lying that misleads the general public.

A class size experiment in the United States found that attending small classes for three or more years, in the early grades increased high school graduation rates of students, from low income families.

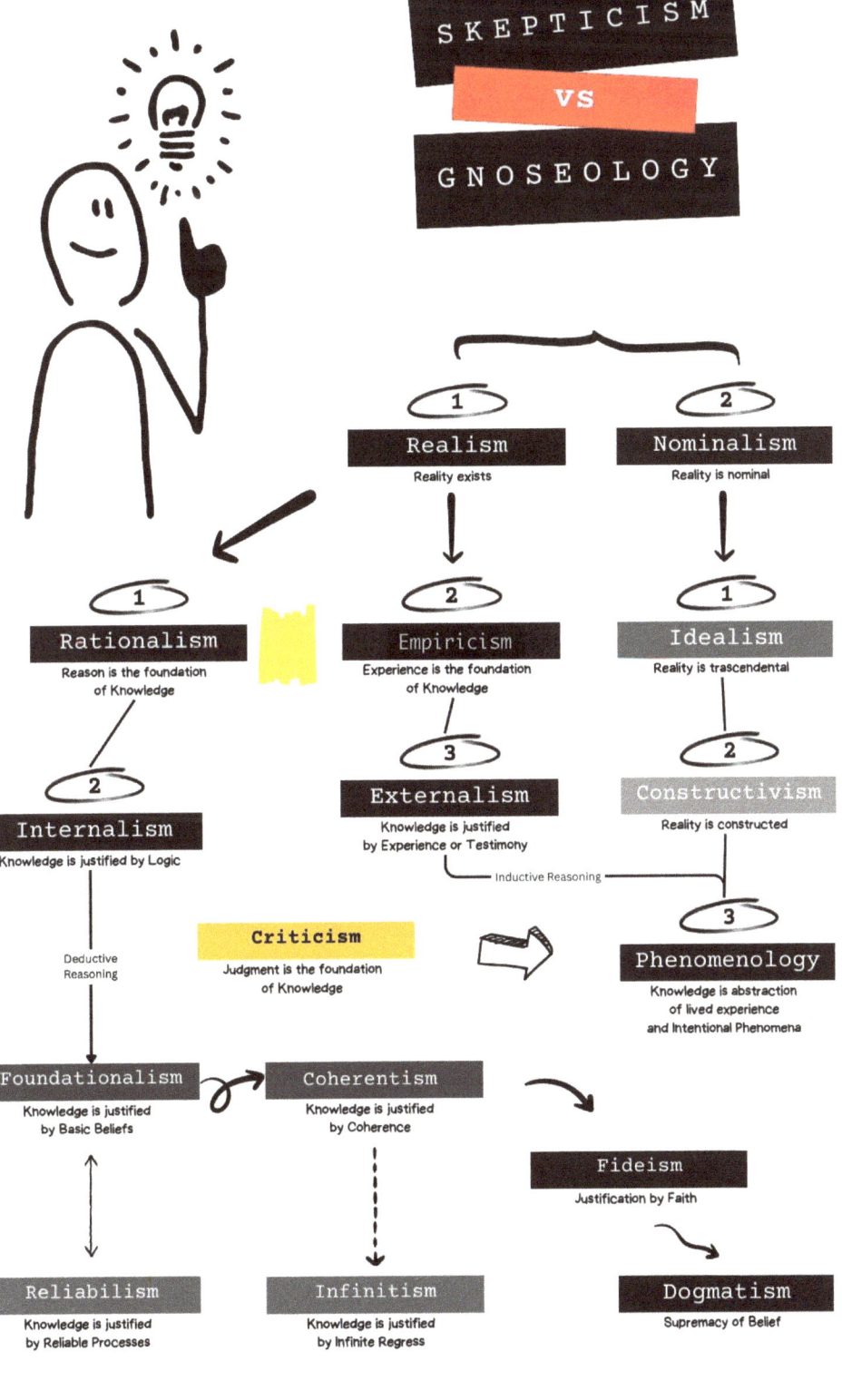

# CHAPTER III

# Logic

## *The Construction of Concepts*

---

What is the only question you can't answer with a yes?
What are numbers and do they really exist?

---

Logic is the study of reasoning and argumentation, observed on a granular level to define the correctness of our inferential thought procedures.

The analysis of the laws and functions that pervade the structure of thought itself (formal logic) is traditionally opposed, in philosophy, to the interpretation of the relationship between thought and its contents (material logic).

Today, logic is understood as a mathematical discipline that studies the forms of deductive reasoning, through the examination of their validity: arguments in which the truth of the conclusions walks behind the premises, regardless of the content of the propositions involved (also called mathematical or symbolic logic).

Arguments are the main object of investigation in logic and consist of a set of propositions, where the truth of one of them, called the *conclusion* is derivable from the validity of the others, called *premises* - in other words, the reality of the conclusion must be justified by the truth of the premises.

To show you what I mean: **(1)** English people are British, **(2)** Londoners are English, **(3)** Londoners are British.

When someone claims to believe $x$, we must first inspect whether that is acceptable or not. To achieve so, there are different methodologies of logical reasoning:

- *deduction*, the gold standard since the classical age;
- *induction*, still subject of criticism;
- *abduction*, recently reevaluated by the philosopher Charles Sanders Peirce.

By giving the argument a logical form, the claimant makes the argument valid or cogent. An argument is said to be logically valid when the connection between the set of premises and the conclusion is exclusively of a logical nature.

Distilled, when the truth of inferences made from premises is valid and thus, the fact corresponds to the real world.

In philosophical language, any type of reasoning that demonstrates the logical achievement of one truth from another, is called inference. To infer is therefore "to draw a conclusion" as handed down from Classical Logic, with the popular *syllogisms*.

To infer $x$ means to conclude that $x$ is true - an inference is the conclusion drawn from a set of facts or circumstances.

An inference is said to be correct or valid if the conclusion is a logical consequence of (i.e., necessarily follows from) premises: if all the premises are true, then the conclusion is necessarily true (or equivalently, it is not possible that the premises are all true and the false conclusion).

Reading top to bottom, from the beliefs to the conclusion, the correct inference rules preserve the truth and avoid suffering clever but false arguments (sophisms).

Review popular inferences with emotionless logic:

> **Correct inference:**
> "If gender is a construct and biological sex is irrelevant, a man with male sex organs who identifies as a woman is a woman already, but if gender is a social construct and biological sex is **not** irrelevant, a man with male sex organs who identifies as a woman is not a woman already. Therefore, if *(A)* gender is a social construct, then *(B)* either biological sex is irrelevant and a man with male sex organs who identifies as a woman is a woman already *(C)* or biological sex is not irrelevant *(-B)* and a man with male sex organs who identifies as a woman is not a woman already *(D)*."

> **Incorrect Inference:**
> "If United Kingdom is a democracy, then Paul refused the Covid-19 vaccine or Dr. Sarah refused to perform abortion. Paul refused the Covid-19 vaccine. So if United Kingdom is a democracy, then Dr. Sarah didn't refuse to perform abortion."

True or False, that is, the values of truth, apply to propositions but not to arguments, while Valid or Invalid (also called fallacious), the logical validity, pertains to arguments and not to propositions.

Ergo, the validity is only a property of arguments, i.e., that they have a good structure; but an argument can be valid, even though its premises are false. What we really want is an argument which is both **(1)** valid and **(2)** and all the statements are true (sound).

The following case is a sound argument, because it contains true premises and the conclusion logically goes after the premises:

- No one under eighteen years old can vote.
- Ryan is under eighteen.
- Therefore, Ryan cannot vote.

Now, the next is a valid argument too since the conclusion logically follows from the premises; however, the first premise is not true. Therefore, this is an unsound argument:

- All cats are pink.
- Toffee is a cat.
- Therefore, Toffee is pink.

An argument may also be unsound when it contains true premises (*All cows are mammals, All dogs are mammals*), but still be invalid since the conclusion doesn't logically follow from the premises (*Therefore, dogs are cows*).

Riddles and brain teasers conventionally challenge humankind and logical thinking engages our mind in seeing patterns, connections.

> There is a man who killed his mother. He was born before his father and married over 100 women, without divorcing any one. Yet, he was considered normal by all of his acquaintances. Why?

You might have to mull over the analytical scaffolding for a few minutes to gather that the mother died from labour, he was born in front of his father and that he was a priest.

English: Carmen is Mexican and a teacher.

First-order logic: $M(c) \land T(c)$

*Formal logic needs to translate natural language arguments into a formal language, like first-order logic, in order to assess whether they are valid. In this example, the colours indicate how the English words correspond to the symbols.*

With reasoning as its focus of attention, logic has consecutively set in motion artificial languages: syllogistic logic (Aristotle), sentential calculus (Boole, De Morgan) to predicate calculus (Russel, Gödel) for the purpose of revealing the underlying sense of natural languages statements like the ones above.

De facto, logic chases the generic meaning of "what concerns the λόγος" (logos), in the multiple sense of "reason" and "speech".

Symbolic writing reflects the ideal structure of a concept, that is a set of premises with a conclusion, in connection (here signified by the sign ⊢).

The identification of the logical form is carried out to successive levels of deepening. The first level is that, of the so-called propositional logic.

Declarative propositions (logic deals only with *logos apophantikos*) follow two principles: the *principle of certainty*, whereby each proposition has one and only one truth value and the *principle of bivalence*, whereby the truth values are only two (True and False); combined together these rules tell us, that each proposition has one - and only one - of the two values of truth.

Truth-functional connectives are named as such, for the propositions formed through them are a function of truth. For instance, in the following, equivalent propositions, A ∨ B → C (A → C) ∧ (B → C), ∨ is a logical disjunct, → is a material implication and ∧ is a logical conjunct.

The truth-tables method is due to Wittgenstein's *Tractatus*, and besides giving us the matrices of the logical connectives, it is a real effective logical calculation system.

By use of this chart, we can mechanically establish the correctness of all propositions and the validity of their resulting argument.

When questioning its foundation (and justification), logic is called the science of [the laws of] thought.

Among these are the *law of identity* (A→A), whereby every proposition implies itself; the *law of non-contradiction* ¬ (A ∧ ¬ A), that no proposition can be both true and false; the *law of excluded middle* A ∧ ¬ A, according to which any proposition must be affirmed or denied.

By assigning one of the two truth values to the propositional variables of a set of words, we calculate the corresponding value assumed by the entire formula, which appears under the main connective.

A formula might take the true value for any truth value assigned to its variables, such would be a tautology. Tautologies are logical laws, for they are always true, by virtue of their logical structure.

| p | q | p ∨ q |
|---|---|-------|
| T | T | T |
| T | F | T |
| F | T | T |
| F | F | F |

**Disjunction Truth Table**
*"If I am 35 years old or if I am 36 years old", then the statement is true. Thus, a disjunction is only false if both propositions are false.*

On the contrary, when a formula assumes the false value, for any truth-value assigned to its elementary constituents, we encounter an inconsistency - the denial of an inconsistency is always a tautology.

A set of expressions is a contingency in a case when, for at least one assignment of truth, values assume the true value and for at least one other assignment, take the false value.

All propositions can belong to *only* one of the three groups. In propositional logic, the only necessary rule of inference is the *modus ponens*, which states in words: if $p$ implies $q$ is a true proposition, and the premise $p$ is also true, then the consequence $q$ is true; in notation with logical operators:

$$[(p \rightarrow q) \wedge p] \vdash q$$

where $\vdash$ represents the logical assertion, also known as *sequent*.

More clearly, considering an argument, the premises must somehow justify the affirmation of the conclusion: they must provide a foundation for the affirmation of the conclusion.

Such justification must - in turn - inevitably be based on a connection between the set of premises and the conclusion: it is for the premises are connected in a certain way to the conclusion, that the premises represent a reason for the affirmation of the conclusion.

In a logically valid argument, the conclusion is logically obtainable, that is, deductible from the premises.

The deducibility consists in the fact that, the conclusion can be drawn through a procedure which does *not* contemplate the intervention of *semantic considerations* on the meaning of the *non-logical terms* that appear in the premises, but which is *entirely* based on *syntactic considerations*, that is, concerning the relationship between the terms; thus, as the terms are related to the non-logical terms, the *meaning of the logical terms*.

The Modus Ponens (MP), literally way that poses with having posed, is a simple and valid rule of inference, basis of an apparently suasive argument for the thesis that, fundamental logical laws can be justified.

In order to prove a *theorem*, that is, to ascertain the truth of one proposition starting from certain premises, you may follow different paths.

Intuition often guides us in the demonstration, but to avoid drawing wrong conclusions, we need be sure that our reasoning is strictly based on correct logical criteria. In the study of geometry, for instance, a real solution is schematized through models, whose reasoning methods, proper to logic, are applied to.

Hence, the enunciative calculation is a reservoir of useful, reasoning principles and may be used as a "model" for the reasoning itself. In other words, tautologies can be used to justify most of the logical laws, in the sense that they constitute the pattern of reasoning used in the proof of any theorem.

Going beyond the level of propositional language, the truth tables are no longer the appropriate tool, therefore it is necessary to implant a *formal system*, that is, an apparatus of rules and principles that allows to check the correctness of the reasoning by building demonstrations in a wholly formal, and mechanical way.

In predicative language, the correctness of reasoning no longer depends on propositional connectives, but rather on quantifiers, and on the structure of straightforward propositions, precisely the connection between subject and predicate.

Frege devised the blueprint for making the propositions universal ("$\forall$") and particular ("$\exists$"), that is, invented the universal and existential quantifiers. Using the quantifiers applied to variables, logic expresses propositions.

For instance, which in natural language is *"someone runs"* becomes $\exists x P(x)$ if $P(x)$ indicates the property of running.

An affirmative universal proposition *(All dogs are mammals)* runs like this: $\forall x\ [A(x) \rightarrow B(x)]$. That is, considering whatever $x$ (for every $x$), if $x$ is a dog (propriety A), then $x$ is a mammal (propriety B).

On the other hand, an affirmative particular proposition *(Some dogs are mordace)* would be: $\exists x\ [A(x) \wedge B(x)]$. There exist, at least one $x$, such that $x$ is a dog (propriety A) and $x$ is biting (propriety B).

Noteworthy, how the affirmative particular proposition is expressed by the congestion *"and"* of the two properties. Lastly, a negative universal proposition *(No dog is a bird)* becomes $\neg \exists x\ [A(x) \wedge B(x)]$. Scilicet, it does not exist, a $x$ such that if $x$ is a dog, be contemporarily a bird.

One of the fundamental problems in logic is the definition of logical constants, that is to say to formulate what unique feature of constants makes them rational, in nature.

A plausible explanation would be that of an invariable, truth-functional logical constructor, that is any element of the *logos* (intended as inference), whose truth-functional nature is essential for the construction of truth itself.

More clearly, symbols such as $\Box$ (necessarily) or $\vee$ (alternation) both qualify the meaning of truth (intension), in the inference, regardless of their denotative form, as satisfying the logical necessity of connotation.

Logical connectives (a type of logical constants) are variable, syntax-qualitative determiners, qualifying the logical relation (the association) between predicates, in the truth-seeking inference.

On the other hand, quantifiers are relative, morphological determiners (a particular form of something) quantifying the propositions, by rapport.

Thus, the point of departure is the distinction between the relations of meaning among predicates, as the need to postulate intensions of predicates in addition to extensions, shapes a legitimate, fruitful way out of the problem of logical constants, wherein statements concerning relations of intent may be formally represented.

After all, the set of elements of any truth - rather than just a few - must be understood for the truth itself to be achieved.

Meaning is the value of *something*, in rapport with the reasons that motivated it or possible consequences; constants bear such importance, indefeasibly leading the logical thrust of an argument.

A major direction to truth we draw out of a summative account of constants is the context, definable as the process of relativization of the study of a specific phenomenon. Context is indispensable for understanding the *real* meaning of a word (or concept), ergo inference depends on its context.

Based on this, Wittgenstein reiterated the instrumentality of the word by declaring that "meaning is use". More functionally, the way the context influences the interpretation of meanings *(situation)*.

On the other extreme, in logic, philosophers grapple with the problem of entailment, which arose from the principle of explosion, that is the issue of whether conditionals carry truth values or not.

The assertion *"If donkeys fly, then the Earth is round"* or symbolically $\neg P \rightarrow (P \rightarrow Q)$ is a contradiction, logically inferring a truth; or $Q \rightarrow (P \rightarrow Q)$ as *verum sequitur ad quodlibet*; $(P \wedge \neg Q) \rightarrow \neg(P \rightarrow Q)$ as *ex vero numquam sequitur falsum*, or lastly $(P \wedge \neg P) \rightarrow Q$ as *ex absurd sequitur falsum*.

In reaction, an axiomatic construction cannot simultaneously satisfy the properties of coherence and completeness. When the whole arithmetic is deduced from the axioms, for instance, there is a contradiction.

Inconsistency in a formal system trivializes the concepts of truth and falsity, like Gödel's incompleteness theorems mandate.

Alternative theories of logic eliminated the *principle of explosion* with inconsistency-tolerant systems, wherein exceptions to the *principle of non-contradiction* may occur in a controlled way; that is, contradictions can arise, without however being able to derive any proposition in the system with this (e.g., paraconsistent logic).

Nonetheless, theoretical positions of this kind do not comfortably translate into the principles of logic.

The deductive method (proper to logic and mathematics) always stems from a postulate or an axiom, that is, from an absolute truth that does not need to be verified - from which it *deduces*, through reasoning, *particular* facts - the validity of what has been shown would collapse, once demonstrated that the initial assertion is false or arbitrary.

Just like that, the premises our reasoning (and the logical foundations) was based on would also collapse. A persuasive invite to abandon formalism, observing how logic is only *sufficiently powerful;* besides *empirically* infeasible for the unaddressed, semantic gaps in its conversion from reality (e.g. irrationality).

As a result, it comes easy to opine, that Hegel may be really the father of contemporary philosophy. Perhaps he was, with its "unpretentious" logic: thesis - antithesis - synthesis; from the synthesis, a new thesis and so on.

Nowadays, antithesis no longer exists; remarkably, in philosophical and mathematical logic, we are in a world that scales forward, in a continuous *thesis-synthesis*.

A clear danger against the onset of a rigorous formal justification for logic, whereby there flourishes an apparent discrepancy between truth and provability or, more precisely, that, under certain hypotheses, *not everything that is true is logically demonstrable*.

# *Is Truth a Logical Possibility?*

---

The day before yesterday, Chris was 7 years old. Next year, he'll turn 10. How's this possible?

---

Those who do philosophy, think and reason. If they think correctly, valid arguments are articulated. Critical thinkers often reflect and affirm theories about what they argue: logic deals with correct reasoning and the validity of arguments in the direction of truth.

The term truth (in Latin *veritas*, in Greek *αλήθεια*) indicates the sense of agreement or coherence with a given or objective reality, or the property of what exists in an absolute sense, and cannot be false.

The question of truth inherent in propositions, affirmations, declarations, ideas, beliefs and judgments refers to the need to identify its foundations.

Each theory of truth can be interpreted both as a definition of the fundamental nature of truth and as a criterion for determining the values of truth.

Realists define truth as correspondence to facts, and conclude that the only valid strategy to establish the truth of a proposition is to check whether the claim corresponds to facts or not.

Hereby, statements made in different languages, such as (in English) "The sky is blue" and (in German), "Der Himmel ist blau" (the sky is blue) are both true and, above all, they are true for the same reason, and that is, for both express the same proposition.

Coherentism differently believes that the truth or falsity of a statement is determined by its consistency within the body of shared, scientific knowledge. Pierce proposed, in his later writings, that truth can be defined as correspondence to reality and that the truth or falsity of a proposition can only be established, through the agreement of experts.

The backbone of the semantic theory of truth is a sentence of the following form:

> "*P*" is true if, and only if, *P*

> "Snow is white" is true if and only if snow is white.

where *P* is the reference to the statement (that is, the name of that statement), and *P* is the statement itself.

The philosopher and logician Alfred Tarski put forward that the semantic theory, for various reasons, could not be applied to any of the natural languages, such as Italian.

Tarski allegedly intended his theory as a particular correspondence theory, where truth is supposed to correspond to facts. He was the elaborator and founder of a semantics of truth, based on "models", whereby the conditions of truth are implied by the components of speech.

Deflationary theories, after Gottlob Frege and F. P. Ramsey, further suggested that "truth" is not the name of any property of propositions - something about which a specific theory can be formulated.

The belief that truth is a property is only an illusion, provoked by the fact that our language predates the predicate "is true", in reference to things, just as if the truth belonged to them.

However, deflationists say, statements that seem to preach the truth only signal a particular concordance with the affirmation itself. For instance, redundancy theory holds that asserting that a certain statement is true is nothing more than asserting the statement itself. Therefore, saying "snow is white" is true, is neither more nor less than saying that the snow is white.

A second bullet is shot by the performative theory, which maintains that saying "snow is white" is true, is simply to perform the linguistic act of signalling one's belief that snow is white. The idea that some sentences are rather "true and real" actions than information is not as strange as it might seem.

To be nimble, when the bride says *"I do"* at the wedding ceremony, she thereby carries out the act of "taking this man to be her rightful husband"; however, she is not describing herself as physically taking this man.

A metalanguage includes primitive notions, axioms, and rules that are absent in the formal language and for this reason, there are provable "theorems" in the metalanguage that are not provable in the natural language.

Quine's thesis of the inscrutability of reference is a launching pad to the idea that there is no way to tell of truth recursively within the statement itself. No language, however richly interpreted, can represent its own semantics and therefore, semantic concepts such as truth cannot be defined in their own language (undefinability of "truth").

> "Noun" is a noun, so it satisfies itself. "Verb" isn't a verb, so it doesn't satisfy itself.

A third type of deflationary theory is the theory "without quotes", which uses a variant of Tarski's scheme: saying that "P is true" is like saying P.

Tarski's formal semantics organizes "the proposition expressed by the sentence", as a criterion that an adequate theory of truth must fulfill: every definition of truth must be both formally correct and materially adequate (material adequacy condition, also known as *Convention T*).

The logician and mathematician bequeathed to linguistic theories the function interpretation, which interprets an expression in a domain

D, a set of well-defined objects. The interpretation function will assign an individual as an extension to a single term, a class to a predicate, and a truth value to a statement.

To talk about truth of a statement it is always necessary to specify both the domain D and the interpretation function I. The same expressions can have different interpretations in different domains, but also in the same domain.

To relax the jargon, whatever we argue about, there are ways things might have been and therefore, there are possible worlds.

Saul Kripke's relational semantics is an evolution of Tarski's formal semantics, where truth depends on "states of things", in alternative worlds to the current one (the possible worlds, accessible from the current one).

Kripke assumed that the names are "rigid designators", that is, they designate the same individual in all possible worlds contemplated by the model structure (albeit, they can label different individuals in the worlds of other model-structures).

Predicates, along atomic statements, change semantic value from one world to another, so that they represent the fact that particular objects could satisfy predicates, other than those they satisfy in the current world.

The fact that from a logical standpoint, we are not required to adopt one in particular (among the infinite model-structures available from theory) helps not to get lost in metaphysical notions on the best map of reality and its possible alternatives.

Equally, the relationship of accessibility between possible worlds can be interpreted with types of relations between objects in the different theories (causal in physics and metaphysics, legal in logic, juridical in law, etc.).

Thus, leading to a unified theory of the various semantics for the systems of alethic, deontic and epistemic logic, with one simple representation through an oriented graph.

The relationship of the starting world with the other worlds accessible by it, is of the Euclidean type.

The transitive property is valid depending on the formal system chosen, if the axiom T or D is valid, it is also symmetric or asymmetrical; never reflective: if from *u* we access *v*, and if always from *u* we access *w*, such passage implies that from *v* we access *w*, that is, the possible worlds are all related to each other.

It follows that since the relationship from the starting world is Euclidean-transitive, those between the possible worlds all enjoy a secondary reflexivity and symmetry (and transitivity).

Different sets of hypotheses give rise to different structures for that language and what Saul Kripke fine-tuned was a semantics for modal logics, bottomed on the concept of possible worlds and the relationship of accessibility between realities.

Yes, logic is an irksome journey. Let me ease the impervious uphill and make his spectacular ideas more easy to reach.

Often we use a name without associating it with any descriptive content specific enough to identify a unique entity. It may as well happen that the object in question is not even the one the name refers to.

Given the failure of Frege's descriptivist theory, Kripke's modal argument holds that the reference to proper names of terms of species ("tiger") or substance ("gold"), as well as the fact that a name N ("Vincent") refers to a human being like me, is never determined by the information associated by speakers of those terms.

In fact, the reference is rather determined by the existence of appropriate causal chains (e.g. my baptism, the mode a name N was transmitted to us, the conformity of a certain community to a type of behavior or rule).

In other words, a name is not synonymous with a defined description, but the description or information associated with a name N are only of service to identify, among real world entities, the entity x to which N refers [convention]; N ("Vincent") then continues to refer to *x* (one person) even when it is used to talk about other possible worlds *y* (another person).

One of the most important logicians of the 20th century, Kripke semantics built truth tables for operators of *possibility* and *necessity*.

**What is Truth? by Nikolai Ge**
*depicting John 18:38, in which Pilate asks Christ "What is truth?"*

Elicited from this semantics, the proposition "It is necessary $p$" is true in a world $w$, if it is true in all worlds $v$ accessible from $w$.

The introduction of that semantics began current studies on modal logics. In symbols, we have the definitions of truth (values 1 or 0) of the two operators, proposed by Carnap in his *"In Meaning and Necessity"*:

$\square\, p \to 1$ (in the current world), if and only if $p \to 1$ (in all) possible worlds

$\square\, p \to 1$ (in the current world), if and only if $p \to 1$ (in some) possible worlds

where *"possible world"* means those accessible from the world chosen as current.

With such drastic field restriction, we no longer account all the alternatives, but only those *possible* for a reference point: the truth or falsity of a modal formula no longer hinges on all possible worlds, but on the relation R of accessibility.

Barcan's formulas affirm an equivalence between necessity (possibility that an object has a certain property) *de dicto* and necessity (possibility that property exists) *de re*.

All in all, a curious analysis of the highly-controversial anagram *"Quid est veritas?"* (from the New Testament, Bible), strikes a compelling dissolution of the long-standing problem of truth, far from logical and semantic smoke.

Reportedly, the question of Pilate did not require an answer from Jesus, for it was implicit in the question.

When you solve the anagram of *"Quid est veritas?"* (what is the truth?), the answer turns out to be: *est vir qui adest* (it's the man, here in front of you).

A towering, self-explanatory postulation in defence of a realist position, beyond all the possible worlds.

Philosophically, a profound distinction pours out between the concepts of [intuitive] truth and the result of a [formal] demonstration.

A contradistinction, after all we discussed, can be imagined by inferring that, not all truths are demonstrable or an infallible machine that produces an infinite number of demonstrations will not reach the whole truth.

Flying in the face of physical and metaphysical standards, logical possibility persists as the weakest sense.

## DID YOU KNOW? ▼

Pythagoras is considered the father of mathematics: he set the foundation for Euclidean Geometry and was the founder of *Pythagoreanism,* a mathematical and philosophical model to map the universe. Markings on animal bones indicate that humans have been doing maths since around 30,000 BC. Most mathematical symbols weren't invented until the 16th century; before that, equations were written in words. The symbol for division (÷) is called an obelus.

Humans do not reason entirely from facts or logic: reason evolved to win arguments (**dialectic**) and people tend to subjectively frame and embrace emotions to support their beliefs, rejecting information that contradicts them (**cognitive bias**).

Mathematics, the science of structure, order and logical reasoning has evolved from elemental practices of counting, measuring to abstraction in idealizing the shapes of objects. Godel demonstrated its **incompleteness**: axioms whose truth or falsehood could not be determined with systematic proof. Formalists like David Hilbert held that mathematics is only a series of games. Intuitionists like L. E. J. Brouwer that numbers, like fairy tale characters, are merely a creation of human mind. Whitehead's type theory too attempted to circumvent the inadequacy of mathematical principles and define it, however retained the flaw of relying on *"logically inconspicuous"* axioms. A rigorous, epistemological justification for the foundations of mathematics is still, quietly, an open problem.

# STUDY OF LOGIC REASONING

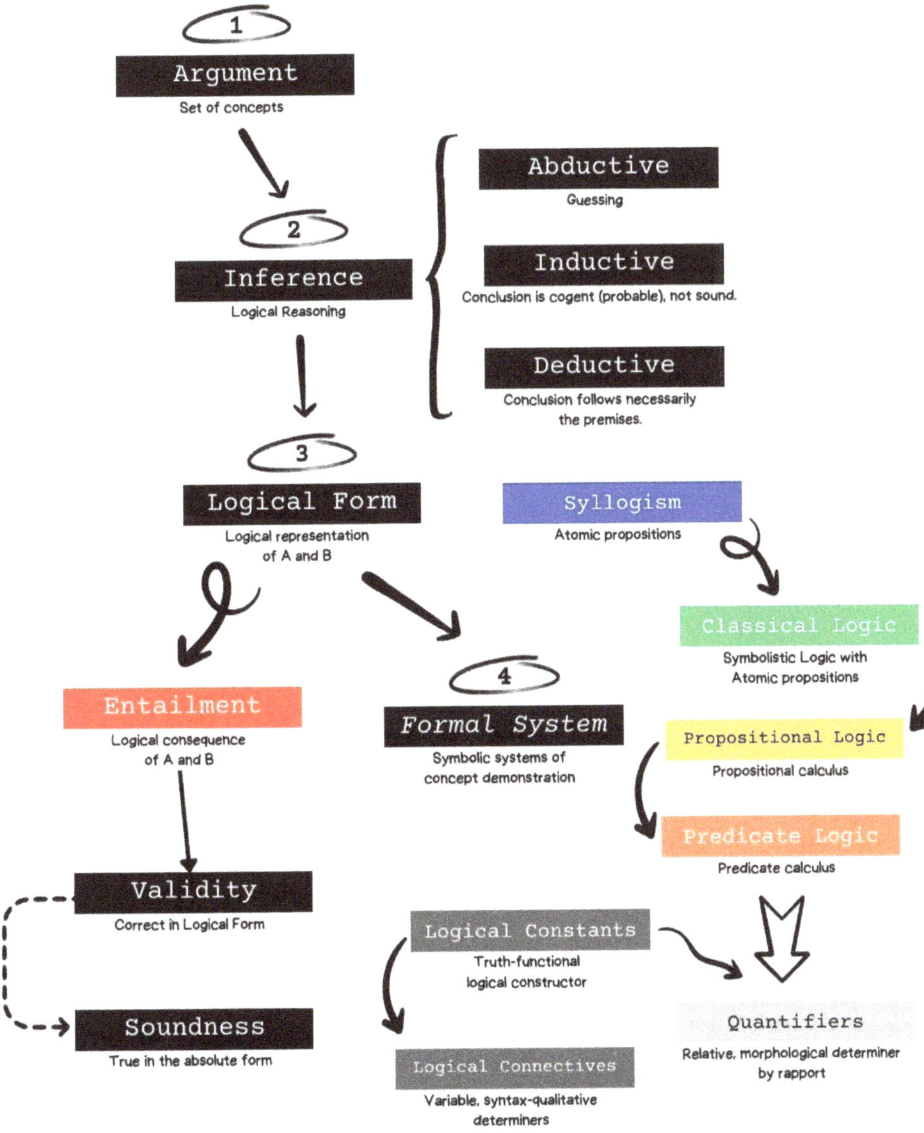

**1. Argument** — Set of concepts

**2. Inference** — Logical Reasoning
- **Abductive** — Guessing
- **Inductive** — Conclusion is cogent (probable), not sound.
- **Deductive** — Conclusion follows necessarily the premises.

**3. Logical Form** — Logical representation of A and B

- **Entailment** — Logical consequence of A and B
  - **Validity** — Correct in Logical Form
  - **Soundness** — True in the absolute form

**4. Formal System** — Symbolic systems of concept demonstration

- **Syllogism** — Atomic propositions
- **Classical Logic** — Symbolistic Logic with Atomic propositions
- **Propositional Logic** — Propositional calculus
- **Predicate Logic** — Predicate calculus

- **Logical Constants** — Truth-functional logical constructor
- **Logical Connectives** — Variable, syntax-qualitative determiners
- **Quantifiers** — Relative, morphological determiner by rapport

# CHAPTER IV

# Morality

## *Aristotle's Ethics.*
## *The Study of Character.*

---

How should we conduct our lives?
A "wrong" act is okay, if nobody ever knows about it.

---

Laying down our rational criteria enables society to assign a deontological status, that is to distinguish human behaviour into good, right, lawful against actions deemed unfair, illicit, inconvenient or bad, with reference to an ideal behavioural model - a given moral.

Ethics is both a set of norms and values that regulate individual conduct in relation to others, and a touchstone of our own and others' actions, with respect to good and evil.

Principles and morality are often used synonymously and in many cases, the manoeuvre is a lawful use, but it is fairer to specify that a difference does exist: morality corresponds to the set of norms and values of an individual or group, whereas ethics, besides sharing this set also entails speculative reflection on those rules, and principles.

Morality accounts norms and values as facts, shared by all, whereas ethics goes all out to give them a rational and logical explanation.

The history of ethics is laminated by the succession of cerebration on humankind and its conduct standards. Philosophers have always reserved considerable space for ethical problems. First in line, Aristotle (who lived between 384 and 322 BC) spent many papers on the issue of ethics and coined the term *etiké theoria* or *techné*. His reflection is remarkable for being both anthropological and ontological.

The most comprehensive works were "*The Nicomachean Ethics*", "*The Eudemian Ethics*" and "*The Magna Moralia*" (also known as "Great Ethics").

Setting aside the questions of authenticity, we can ascribe Aristotle's works to a standard framework, because the main themes are always addressed in the same sequence:

- The concept of the *Supreme Good* and *Happiness*
- The e*thical virtue* in general and ethical virtues, in particular
    - *Dianoetic* or intellectual virtues
    - The *vices*, the lack of self-control
- *Friendship* (characterised by utility, pleasure, and virtue)
- The *perfect virtue*, the *complete happiness*

The purpose of Aristotelian ethics is the teleological realization of what is good for the individual (*ethikē aretē*): Aristotle dismissed that the aim of ethics is the achievement of absolute good as Plato intended it (with the idea of the Supreme Good, the principle of reality and the world of ideas), ergo, extraneous to the practical life of people.

Rather, in his eyes, the Supreme Good is pigeonholed as within the reach of humankind with the achievement of *eudaemonia* - happiness - which can only be achieved when such is self-sufficient; happiness, for starters, cannot be wealth, since that is a means to be used for other purposes.

Aristotle looks on happiness as something desirable for itself, and that is only "human's own work (or activity)", meaning, the exercise of that faculty which characterizes people; the rational activity, a practical effort following reason that, come what may, brings happiness only when carried out excellently. For humans, hence, happiness is the excellent exercise of cognitive and practical works of reason.

The Platonic idea whereby the good of the single is the absolute good - the being - vanished with Aristotle's thesis; ethics is no longer the science of being, rather the science of becoming.

Hereupon, Aristotle pigeonholed the foundation of ethics as "autonomous practical knowledge". He is, thus, an ethical cognitivist like Kant. Philosophy, by consequence, must train human beings in its discovery of "the way to act" so as to achieve good.

The Nicomachean Ethics is not intended as a reading for young people, usually those carried away by passions and lacking experience, deemed necessary to understand the work; preferably, the work is aimed at those who already possess the virtues but are unable to make a moral choice. The disquisition starts precisely from the concept of *praxis*, since ethics itself is inherent in it.

Aristotle led off wondering what is good for human beings, what is ευδαιμονια (generally translated as "happiness", but perhaps this is a somewhat reductive translation).

The good for people is *"that which everything, by nature, tends to"*. To Aristotle, everything is in constant evolution for each thing evolves, labouring to reach the higher aim to the position where that is, hence each one tends to an ultimate end which is its own natural purpose: everything tends to fulfil itself, to be itself.

Eudaimonia is a state of grace that allows individuals to express their full potential. Aristotle supplied a coherent account with metaphysics, through the idea that activity empowers to realize the *potentiality* of an individual. The metaphor is that of the flourishing, that is, of what - in the seed - is only *in potential*.

Such unification of one's existence to a rational and sensible narrative is an asset that plays a major role, at the present time, in analogy to Aristotle's eudaimonia; in other words, eudaimonia can be interpreted as a "theory of identity", defining the concept of good life as the *telos* - the best every human action tends to.

Commentators further pumped Ἀριστοτέλης's interpretation of flourishing and added that such end never transcends the individuals, nor is external to the latter, but that is, on the contrary, immanent in the vicissitudes of their psychic life.

Acting by virtue is not to be accepted as performing well the task that is proper to the human being *in general*, rather such is to be understood as performing well the task of maintaining the integrity of one's identity, in the plurality of situations, and inscribe its salient features in an unrepeatable biography. In this perspective, Aristotle's ontological coherence is manifest, when eudaimonia becomes life cycle.

The good life (or eudaimonia) in a postmodern sense - the life cycle wherein people can enrich the main plot of their own life story with the broadest number of episodes and secondary strands - dovetails with the maintenance of an overall unity.

The ethics Aristotle engineered is concerned with the sphere of behaviour (from Greek *ethos*): the conduct to be followed in order to live a happy existence. Consistent with its philosophical architecture, the most correct attitude is the one that produces the essence of everyone (welfare).

Being is identified with value: the more an entity fulfils its *raison d'être*, the more the entity is worth. People, in particular, fulfil themselves by practicing three forms of living: the hedonistic one, focused on body care, the political one, based on the social relationship with others, and the theoretical life, above all the others, which has contemplative knowledge of truth, as its ultimate aim.

These three modes of behaviour must be integrated with each other, without giving preference to one, to the detriment of the other. Even more so, human beings must know how to develop and harmoniously support all three potentialities of the soul that distinguish their own being or *entelechy*, identified by Aristotle with the vegetative soul, the sensitive soul and the rational soul.

On the back of the tripartition, the Greek philosopher identified pleasure and health as the purpose of the vegetative soul, resulting from the balance between opposing excesses; for instance, avoiding eating too much or too little.

Aristotle allocated the soi-disant ethical virtues to the sensitive soul, which are behavioural habits acquired by training reason to dominate impulses, in the search for the "right means" between extreme passions; for example, courage is the median attitude to be preferred between cowardice and recklessness. Since individuals are "social animals", balance is what must guide one's relationships with others; these must be based on the correct recognition of the honours and prestige deriving from the exercise of public office. The different ethical virtues are, therefore, all encapsulated in the virtue of *justice*.

For Plato, justice was the harmony between the faculties of the soul and between the classes of citizens, inasmuch that it attributes to each faculty or to each social class what each one is entitled to, as a *fulfilment of their own task* (ta autou prattein).

Aristotle amplified and repaired the Pythagorean idea of equality: justice participates in the essence of virtue and should represent the right means between a defect, and an excess.

In Book V of the *Nicomachean Ethics*, the Stagira native, however, opposed injustice to justice by appraising justice, as a particular virtue and developing the concept of "mediumness" to refer to two extreme quantities (too much and too little), in the assignment of honours, and public goods or in the private exchange of goods.

With Aristotle, the means of justice, in the strict sense, concurs with the equal, and is not measured by a fixed quantity, like for Pythagoras, rather it is variable. It is not a matter of giving everyone in the same way, but of giving each one their own. The distinction between distributive justice and commutative justice is traced back to this postulation; the first regulates public relations (distribution of honours and public wealth), the other controls private relations (exchange of things).

In the history, the Aristotelian naturalistic theory of justice as equality is set against justice as freedom - with Kant - whose equality is the objective, formal limit.

To the rational soul, Aristotle earmarked the so-called dianoetic virtues, divided into calculative and scientific. Calculating faculties have a practical purpose, they are tools in view of something else: art (téchne) has a productive purpose, wisdom or prudence (phrònesis) is of use to direct ethical virtues, as well as to coach political action. If these virtues are to be pursued in view of a higher good, however, there must still be a good to be pursued for itself, in the end.

The scientific faculties, aiming at selfless knowledge of the truth, do not have any other goal beyond wisdom in itself (sophìa). The two cognitive faculties of knowledge contribute to that supreme virtue: science (epistème), which is the ability of logic to execute demonstrations and intelligence (noùs), which dispenses the first principles those demonstrations arise from.

*Allegory with a portrait of a Venetian senator (Allegory of the morality of earthly things), attributed to Tintoretto, 1585*

Arguably the most influential philosopher ever, Aristotle instituted the concept of knowledge as a "lifestyle", disconnected from any practical purpose; whilst representing the natural inclination of all human beings, only philosophers fully fulfil an absolutely free knowledge, by implementing a knowledge that has no purpose, but equally for this reason they will not bow to any servitude.

Contemplation of truth is therefore an activity in itself, happiness (eudaimonìa) properly lodges in, and it is what marks people from other animals, making them more similar to God - already defined by Aristotle as «thought of thought», pure self-sufficient reflection, that nothing must seek outside of itself.

Aristotle triggered a fundamental distinction between ethical virtues and dianoetic virtues: ethical virtues are those of the *orexis*, the desiring and passionate zone; dianoetic virtues are those obtained through teaching, ergo their space is that of school and theoretical knowledge.

The peripatetic held *phronesis* to be fundamental, for prudence is knowledge which becomes action and only phronesis, by becoming *habitus* (or moral disposition) let people not only discern the goals to be pursued, moreover to identify the means by which to achieve them.

Plato argued that the immortality of the soul was the true subject of moral happiness for human beings; his student rejected the notion of the soul as individually immortal.

The reward for those who act well is, for Aristotle, happiness in this life and in this world and, as a consequence, there will be no further pain and punishment for those who act badly than unhappiness in this life, and in this world.

The Greek philosopher also criticized his teacher for his idea that the good is something common: every form of knowledge, every praxis, each choice is oriented towards their specific purpose; given that the good is "which that everything tends to", the factual multiplicity of this tendency distributes an equally, irreducible multiplicity of purposes, and therefore, of goods.

Impossible is to speak of good in a unitary sense, except by analogy, in the sense of a common underlying position that designates what constitutes the goal of each individual-oriented action.

De facto, Aristotle argues that there are three types of good: the good itself, meaning the eudaimonia; the good for another, that is, an effect desired in function of another aim, thus such good breeds a *means* rather than a real aim; and the universal good, of the many, of the citizens of the *polis*, which is worth more than the single good, hence politics marries the search for the good of all.

The correlative concept of vice brings forward its eternal antithesis, virtue, especially because the moral deviance expressed by vices is selected as connected to the same primitive, evil nature of the individual.

While virtue is inspired by a true idea of happiness that extends to common good, Aristotle set forth, vice is based on a false formulation of happiness which, inferred selfishly, then, causes social injustice.

Vices, like virtue, shoot from the repetition of actions, which form, in the subject who performs them, a sort of "habit", a "second nature", that points the same towards a habit that - in the case of vice - does not promote an inner, noble and spiritual growth, alas on the contrary, deteriorates it.

A good education is beyond peradventure needed, comprehensive of punitive tools, to shepherd youngsters to the formation of good "habits" and a virtuous, excellent character.

Aristotle does not completely mandate virtue but clarifies that its "state" is not sufficient - "activity" (power and act) is necessary to achieve the flourishing.

One may easily ponder, at this crossroads of reflection, if Aristotle's positive regard of human beings was too lenient.

## *Ethics and Moral in Hume.*
## *A Contemporary Reading.*

---
Is it essential to be a "good person"?

---

Through the philosophy of the thinker David Hume, everyday, parts of the world impose legal codes with the vision of a distorted justice, alleging social utility but in fact, generated by those feelings - a bundle of sensations - for the British philosopher, inherent in all human actions.

Probably the most radical of the three, great British empiricists (the other two being John Locke and George Berkeley), Hume criticized the instrument of reason for being not as effective as it is thought.

The moral that Immanuel Kant trumpeted through the Enlightenment - crediting Hume as the inspiration for awakening him from "dogmatic slumbers" - is a brown study on the right act of people, without ignoring the rules dictated by reason. Ethics to be right must follow the paths of reason, and that is still reason, just not theoretical-speculative but practical.

Kant invented the concept of categorical imperative where a behaviour is to be viewed as categorically moral "without the possibility of denial", when that is universally recognized - right at all times and in every human situation. This conduct becomes binding on the morals of all people, and their failure to apply it would mean immoral action.

With the German philosopher seeking the foundation of morality in an unconditional command, the jurist Bentham purveyed the principle whereby "it is the greatest happiness of the greatest number that is the measure of right and wrong" - the fundamental axiom of modern utilitarianism. All these doctrines are logical outcomes of Hume's empiricism.

The latter philosopher began to stalk the epistemological limits of reason and traced its boundaries, outlining what is not within its competence, as something related to the "sentiment" or "impression". In line with his attack on the role that reason had created in previous centuries, Hume argued that moral also falls outside the scope of reason.

Morality is, as he put it, a "matter of fact, not of abstract science" and therefore unknowable in its essence from reason; moreover, it follows autonomous trails from reason.

The highest criticism Hume moved to morality is that of being conditioned by external events that would try to say *a priori* what is right and what is wrong (religion is one of these influences).

In the concrete, the goodness of an action is (and must be) completely independent of a promised prize and the fear of a penalty.

The British empiricist all the more evinced that knowledge of human nature should be observed by means of experience.

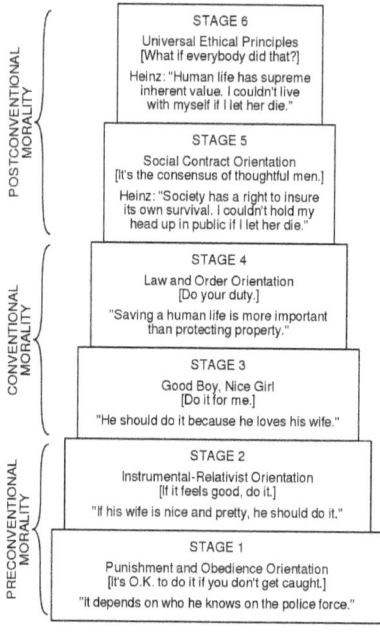

**Kohlberg's model of moral development**
*Morality evolves by virtue of another feeling, that of sympathy, when we feel close to our fellows and share happiness, and unhappiness.*

Knowledge should be entrusted to the analysis of sentiment rather than reason and morality itself, imbued with religious and abstract ideals, must be studied on naturalistic grounds.

One step closer, moral standards do not even have immutable and eternal laws but invariably spring out of *impressions*, which generate sympathy for people belonging to the society where we live, when we feel close to them in happy or difficult moments.

For Hume, hence, morality is a problem of sensations and passions that constitute any human action, unlike those who supposed that reason constitutes every mechanism of our actions.

Hume was of the opinion that reason is "perfectly inert" and "wholly inactive", that our intellect has only the "true" and the "false" as its object, never the [morally] "good" and "evil".

Actions may only be "laudable" or "blameworthy", but never "reasonable" or "unreasonable". What someone does only depends on their feelings or passions, and the task of reason is limited to demonstrating their object to feelings and showing the passions, the ways to their satisfaction.

It is lapalissadian, for the Scottish philosopher, to gasp at how we can get to the concept of "duty": he forbid to deduce from an "Is" an "Ought", thus overcoming the "naturalistic paralogism".

People are led to feel the sentiment of benevolence, in social context, when it comes to virtuous acts, whereas we move away in fierce disdain for morally bad ones.

This is the cornerstone of the entire Hume's theory of morality and justice, where actions are always set up on feelings and - the Edinburgh native would elaborate - on *social utility*, seen as the criterion for any moral evaluation.

The "circumstance of public utility is always what is considered to be the main", for the feeling of benevolence is closely linked to human interests. Hence, justice arises from the need to uphold and benefit useful interests to society. In the event that we do not need anything else that would favour social profits, and if we were all endowed with benevolence, justice would be entirely useless.

As a classical utilitarian, Hume rightly constructed a connection between morality and sentiment. Reason may only control the irrationality of an impulse, unable to manage passions, consequently it only has a descriptive function, not a prescriptive one; and in fieri, utility interlays as the measure of happiness for a sensitive being.

At the time, such *moral algebra* or "happiness calculation" was a highly accomplished formulation, in ethical contexts, by Jeremy

Bentham, who silhouetted utility as what minimizes pain, produces advantage and maximum pleasure.

His thought proselytized John Stuart Mill who, keeping the analysis at individual level, would subsequently relativize the amount of pleasure to the individual's degree of refinement.

Utility, therefore, became the pivot of ethical reasoning, and its direct application is that different social states (in the sense of *welfare state*) are comparable, with respect to the level of global utility generated by them, intended as an aggregation of the grade of utility achieved by the individuals.

Aim of justice is the maximization of social well-being, therefore the maximization of the sum of individual utilities, by the well-known Benthamian motto:

> "The maximum of happiness for the maximum number of people."

Utilitarianism is a theory of justice whereby it is "right" to perform the act that, among the alternatives, increases overall happiness, measured by utility.

Irrelevant are the notes about the morality of an act - or the dutifulness - nor the supererogatory ethics; there is no *a priori* moral judgment.

Murder is a representative case: the act can be considered "right" as soon as that results in a social status, with greater total utility, namely killing a terrorist. In point of fact, it may occur that a single individual lost utility from his own death, when the other members of the community would gain, in utility, from his demise.

Granted that, utilitarianism is attributed a *consequentialist* view of justice (otherwise called end-state oriented or non-a priori): the justification of a choice is subject to the result (in terms of utility-happiness) that it entails for sensitive beings.

The only, a priori assumption of utilitarianism is impartiality: the various utilities of each individual are summed up, to form the utility of the social state, without weights of weighting. In other words, every contingent situation, every point of view has equal value in the function of aggregating social well-being.

When "right" is what maximizes utility, an allocative vision of justice results: justice is the efficient management of social utility.

Nodal are the Humean elements that converge to make up personal merit, alias, those characteristics that make human beings - in general sense - worthy of esteem or contempt: the moral problem becomes a matter of fact.

Through the distinction between natural (self-love and benevolence) and artificial virtues (obligations governing property, justice and government, or the chastity of women to make society cohesive), Hume built a bridge between politics and economy.

Utility is fundamental for the social life of the subjects' moral qualities: for Hume, good is what is pro everyone, evil what damages society.

There is, ad hoc, the feeling of sympathy, understood as an interest in humanity. Sympathy derives from the Greek *sympatheia* and refers to "suffering together", "sharing the emotion", "feeling the emotion with someone".

What separates a virtue from a vice is the impression that generates. When the impression is pleasant, then it is a virtue; if it is unpleasant, then it is a vice. In Hume's moral philosophy, there is no place for perpetual and unchanging moral standards.

Ergo, the concept of free will has strong ethical implications, being the basis of responsibility, without whom an individual could not respond for their actions.

From the incomprehensible idea of a person with a "lawless" free will - a will that acts without any causal structure - Kant lit on a free will that acts under laws the same gives to itself.

Like you, Hume too noticed the obvious conflict between determinism and free will, how it is not possible to be free to choose, if actions have already been determined for billions of years. Further, philosophers knew this loophole would drive the whole moral dilemma to a paradoxical outlet: free will is incompatible with indeterminism.

Since your actions were not determined by past events, then they would be completely accidental and henceforth disconnected from your character, your desires, preferences, values, etc. As a result, we cannot be responsible for actions that do not depend on our character and there is no reason for anyone to be held responsible, before the law for actions which, as we have just concluded, are aleatory.

In contemporary perspectives, Hume appears to offer a compelling account of justice (morality) and "inert reason", because society is still, by and large, moved by a moral sense close to its deepest passions and feelings (psychological hedonism).

Despite excellent health and love, most people these days, frustrated by a boring routine and aesthetic alienation, chase a new source of pleasure to inspire them to morally contribute and change the world.

Sad to relate, these feelings and status anxiety have the whip hand to make the generational cohorts degenerate into an unbridled ambition without compromise, crying to assert their superiority over others.

The psychology behind human behaviour alone affords a great deal of philosophical reflections on justice and morals, potentially related to David Hume's view of human nature: whether true justice descends from reason or equity has its origins from the motions of feelings and passions, and if moral utility is the true foundation of social morality.

Remarkable is the historical reference to moral weakness and evil men, in the state of nature. Used for the first time by Aristotle, the term *akrasia* properly stands for the lack of ethical force (*a-kratos*, absence of force), which echoes our contemporary inertia, in Hume's concept of reason.

Inability to dominate one's bodily self followed by an action contrary to the moral beliefs of the subject, akrasia assumes different physiognomies in ancient thought, which vary through the definitions that the interpreters give to the logos, passions and combined play of both.

Euripides was the first to stage what Aristotle later coined with the term *akrasia*, that lack of self-domination which leads people to act against what is believed to be the best way; these are the first attempts at beating the archaic conception of justice, which did not take into account the agent's intentions, as we do now but judged only the action carried out in itself.

Assuming the similarity with the concept of inert reason in Hume and contrasting an akratic deduction of human nature such as that of *"Homo Homini Lupus"*, a definitive conclusion caught the eye with multi-disciplinary findings: human being is a social animal.

Animated by a strong feeling of emotional sharing (sympathy), people tend by nature to look for others who feel - like them - analogous feelings, before analogous situations.

To give his thesis impetus, Hume borrowed an equally ancient concept expressed by Terenzio, *"Homo sum, humani nihil a me alienum puto"*, whereby nothing of what is human is foreign to the individual self.

In practice, another congenital peculiarity in people, along with sympathy, is therefore empathy, that is, the ability to fully comprehend the mood of others.

Sympathetic and empathetic beings, individuals, by their *very* nature, seek community, to be understood as a collective of like-minded individuals.

Our reality and these facts insinuate that human beings are animals and, as such, dominated by passions, yet without confrontation and the awareness of being able to find another, before us - who we could share sufferings and joys - we cannot live.

All in all, human connection is a social pillar of individuals, and of morality undergirded by a basic need to live in a group that can share feelings and thus, understand each other's successes or failures.

At this century stop, the ethical search for individual utility has obsessively become social, as the only, fundamental "reason" for any human behaviour.

## DID YOU KNOW? ▼

It's illegal to ride an ugly horse in Wilbur, Washington and in Kalispell, Montana, children must have a doctor's note if they want to buy a lollipop.

In Eureka, Nevada, it is illegal for men who have moustaches to kiss women and flirting in Little Rock, Arkansas, can land someone in jail for 30 days.

The Byzantine emperor Justinian's sixth-century compilation of Roman law *Institutiones* became the foundational source for Roman law in the Western tradition. All later systems of law in the West borrowed heavily from it including the civil law systems of Western Europe, Latin America and parts of Africa, and to a lesser but still notable extent the English common law system. The original compilation consisted of three different parts: the Digest (*Digesta*), the Code (*Codex*) and the Institutes (*Institutiones*). The Digest (533 CE) collected and summarized all of the classical jurists' writings on law and justice. The Code (534 CE) outlined the actual laws of the empire, citing imperial constitutions, legislation and pronouncements. The Institutes (535 CE) were a smaller work that summarized the Digest, intended as a textbook for students of law.

# CHAPTER V

# Ethics

## *Objectifying Morality*

---

Is it objectively wrong to torture innocent babies just for fun?
Is morality relative?

---

Morality is the set of ideal values or principles, the individual and the community freely conform their choice of behaviour to.

Moral reasoning focuses on normative judgments by prescribing what is mandatory or right to do. Moral judgments tell us what we should do in situations where our own demands or those of several people are in conflict with each other.

Ethics is, therefore, both a set of norms and values that regulate one's behaviour in relation to others, and a criterion that allows one to judge its own and others' behaviour, with respect to good and evil.

In his *Principia Ethica*, Thomas Moore takes it upon himself to rigorously analyze moral language and to define the meaning of properly moral concepts (such as good, duty, mandatory). By making a distinction between moral and ethical life, Moore glossed:

> "Ethics does not constitute any form of knowledge: it only has to do with emotions, recommendations and prescriptions."

Without providing a direct answer to genuinely moral questions and focusing entirely on their justification, metaethics studies the reasons and original principles (objectivity) of morality, across three main areas.

In the first place, by questioning the semantics (meaning) of moral expressions; for instance, which object of thought can designate the word "good" (G. E. Moore 1903) or in recent debate, whether saying "torturing animals is wrong" expresses a belief that can be true or false as opposed to the expression of a *conative* state (desire) - that animals not be tortured.

The metaethical theory known as "cognitivism" holds that ethical sentences express propositions and can, therefore, be true or false, that is, they would have true value (truth-bearers).

Ethical cognitivism encompasses moral realism (which states that ethical sentences express propositions about facts, independent of the mind in the world) and its form of ethical naturalism (moral judgments are reducible to factual and empirical judgments of a scientific type) and non-naturalism (formulated by G. E. Moore's open question argument, arguing no moral property is equal to a natural property such as pleasure or God, for most are intuitive).

At the other end of the stick, non-cognitivism denies the cognitivist claim that "moral judgments are capable of being objectively true, because they describe some feature of the world". Informally, the main function of moral sentences is not to state any fact whatsoever but rather to express an evaluative attitude towards an object of evaluation (expressivism).

Philosophers from A. J. Ayer to Hare, Blackburn to Simmons argue that moral judgments do not have a cognitive value, rather they are projections of emotions and feelings, thus lead and determine [condition] to act morally (emotivism); moral statements function like universalized imperative sentences (universal prescriptivism), as though they were linguistically *real* (quasi-realism).

Along the same bricks of moral anti-realism, ethical subjectivism upholds that ethical sentences express propositions about people's attitudes or opinions, while error theory argues that ethical sentences exhibit propositions, but that they are all false, whatever their nature.

In the second place, metaethics inquires the *metaphysics of moral expressions* (ontology), probing whether there are moral properties in the world - independent from the human stand to justify the correctness of some moral judgments, with reference to others (objectivity) - or moral expressions do nothing but project fictitious entities into a world, made up only of non-evaluative properties (subjectivity).

**Eduard von Grützner's depiction of Falstaff**
*A literary character well known for his joie de vivre.*

Moral universalism (also called moral objectivism) swears that a system of ethics or universal ethics applies *universally*, for "all individuals in the same situation"; Kant notoriously attempted to derive a supreme principle of morality that binds all rational agents.

The existence of universal values is unproven conjecture of moral philosophy (and beyond, such as aesthetics), although it is clear that certain values are shared by a great diversity of people (value monism), though sometimes goods are incompatible to each other (value pluralism).

Relativism in morality is known as moral relativism, a philosophical stance opposed to the existence of universal moral values.

This differs from cultural relativism, in that the latter, only describes the fact that there are cultures with different moral codes, whereas the former postulates that there is no universal morality, for all morality is relative to a certain system of values.

Moral relativism (or broadly speaking, skepticism) at its best, is moral nihilism, the metaethical thesis that nothing is morally right or wrong.

Many people are convinced that they know what is right and what is wrong but, in reality, objectivity as a universal agreement is not an easy decision to make.

It follows that, metaethics ultimately questions moral epistemology; for instance, if we know that killing is wrong on the basis of empirical observation (naturalism) or rather, on the authority of some form of *a priori* intuition (intuitionism).

Objectivist principles include rationalism, alias, reason as the guide of human actions and the right to exist for oneself (individualism), without the obligation to sacrifice for morality - altruism is coercively immoral - the pursuit of happiness as the purpose of existence (eudaimonia) and the conception of the human being as a heroic being (Ubermensch).

Since moral rationalism contemplates reason and the empirical sciences as an absolute value, metaphysics is also accepted as real.

Reality, however, is based on the benevolent universe: if people live by morality and adapt to the laws of the universe, they will have a greater chance of success (constructive egoism).

Rand's conception of the intangibility of the core of individual human rights (negative freedom) also known as *property rights* is typically liberal.

Moral subjective and cognitivist claims of this vein are heavily contrasted by Hume, with his *Is-Ought Problem (*or Moore's *naturalistic paralogism*) who reckoned the logical leap between propositions indicating facts (is) and propositions indicating values (ought), an error.

Empiricists rate experience (emotions) is essential [practical] in determining morality and immorality, the only foundation of knowing from the objective vantage point. Yet the latest discredit, in order of time, is traceable to quantum mechanics, whose experiments reiterate there is no such thing as objective.

If at all, morality can be said to be objective only if it takes into account "human nature", enduring that such is inseparable from culture. In philosophical style, objectivity requires a moral ontology of human subjectivity.

## *Ethical Demands*

> Free Will, then we can Kill.

Normative ethics watches the foundations that make it possible to assign a *deontological* status to human behaviours, that is to distinguish them into good, right, licit, as reported by ideal, behavioural models (justice, good).

The flux of normative ethics fends off the *ethics of virtue* (bringing the moral evaluation on agents), *deontology* (morally evaluating actions conforming to their respect for imperative norms) and *consequentialism* (morally evaluating actions depending on whether or not, they help to improve the state of the world).

At the nadir of each ethical concept lies the notion of good and evil, of virtue and a specific vision of human relationships.

Based on the teleological theory (finalism), an act is "right", if and only if such (or the norm wherein it falls) produces, will produce or *probably* will produce a prevalence of good over evil - at least, inasmuch as any other accessible alternative.

The deontological theory, by contrast, holds that the modalities of the action are the action itself, that is, in evaluating an action we cannot ignore the intent of the agent. It follows that the duty and the intention are placed before the purpose of the action.

The basic judgments of obligation are all and only particular, therefore, the general judgments are unusable, useless or derive from particular judgments (deontological theory of the act).

Another deontological philosophy (called the *deontological theory of the norm*) argues, otherwise, that the code of right and wrong consists of one or more norms and, therefore, norms are valid, regardless of whether they promote good or not.

These norms are basic and do not flow *by induction* from particular cases.

The question whether good is a priority over right has permeated ethics for centuries and feeds a prolific, multi-disciplinary back-and-forth. Liberalism recognized certain autonomy of the "right" with respect to the "good"; it is a duty to act [conform] to a right norm, on the basis of the principles of justice (Locke, Kant, Nozick).

For communitarianism, justice is not about rules and procedures, but something that concerns the behaviour of people with respect to their peers - justice is a virtue of the person.

Charles Taylor, in the other room, pledged that it is illusory to imagine the "right" can be separated from reference to the "good". There is a primacy of "good" over "right", where good does not mean utility, rather "everything that stands out over other things, by virtue of a qualitative distinction".

Morality does not concern only public obligations and rules, but represents, first of all, qualitative distinctions.

**Cardinal and Theological Virtues by Raphael, 1511**

The ethics of virtues necessitated a dialogue, since morality stands on internal features of the person - the *virtues* - in contrast to the position of deontology, whereby morality comes from *rules* or consequentialism, where morality kicks from the result of an act (utility).

The difference between those three ways to morality resides more in the reasons, *moral dilemmas* such as euthanasia, abortion or suicide are approached by (e.g. bioethics) than in the value reached.

Throughout its history, morality has been concerned with cultivating certain inclinations of human beings, amongst which *character* and *virtue* certainly stick out. Virtues are dispositions or traits, not entirely innate. They must be acquired, at least in part, through the continuous learning and practice of these teachings.

As we've seen, for Hume, the will absolutely cannot be moved by rules: reason is unable to found morality, thus the foundation of morality is *sentiment*.

In his frame of reference, morality is conceived primarily as the acquisition and cultivation of those traits, alias, making virtues a real *habitus*.

In the ethics of virtues, morality is based on aretaic judgments, not deontic principles (*areté*, "virtue or excellence"). Deontic principles (rules) derive from aretaic ones (virtues) and if they do not, they are deemed superfluous.

Early philosophers set the table for moral reflection, with the concept of *responsibility*. The term generally hints at a behaviour being attributed to an agent but the problem lies in establishing under what conditions, it is correct to judge an agent or hold one responsible for an action.

Aristotle argued someone is responsible, if the cause of the action is internal to the subject (not forced to act) or the act is not the result of ignorance (consciousness of action).

Determinists would add that one's personal, social and political choices are always conditioned; case in point, responsibility as a wilful commitment became accountability, whereby a subject can be called to respond [be liable] for the culpable or wilful violation of a standardized obligation.

That being said, moral values account for the object of ethics: to describe the criteria that allow human beings to judge their own behaviour (or consequences) and that of others (descriptive ethics).

Axiology researches the values that people deem as worthy, referring to an ideal, metaphysically-charged hierarchy, humankind must aspire to climb as high as possible.

Utilitarianism promotes the principle of *utility* as the ultimate criterion, whereby the moral purpose in everything we do, is the greatest possible remnant of good over evil.

In normative ethics, utility always highlights the centrality of norms and asserts that usually, if not always, we must establish what to do in particular situations, by appealing to them.

For act utilitarianism, an agent's act is morally correct if and only if, it produces the best possible results in that specific situation. Conversely, for rule utilitarianism each agent must wonder about what would happen, if everyone did so, in such cases (universizability); therefore, the act is morally correct if and only if, such yields the maximum utility.

Martin Luther believed that occasional minor evil could have a positive effect

Notoriously, values originate from social and political reality (pragmatic ethics), therefore "what is a crime in England could be praiseworthy in Algiers". Further, they mirror the economic and legal organization (situational ethics), within the traditions of a community and therefore, change along their historical path. Consequentialism assumes an ambivalent, intimate and collective nature and this is the reason why, across time, it embedded another normative institution: the law.

Ethics and law do not coincide, yet there are multiple convergence points: the *common sense* and the fundamental principles of law established in the Universal Declaration of Human Rights, a reference point for every State obliged to form the legal systems, following those principles (State consequentialism).

Contractualism is a constructivist attempt at providing a unified account of the moral values and responsibility, that is, morality is based on a contract or social agreement - which Scanlon calls "what we owe to each other".

The application of ethical principles to real-world situations and issues keeps breeding complications, with no minimal controversy. Contemporary puzzles in practical ethics came to light when normativity hit personal domains like abortion, euthanasia, genetic engineering, climate change, animal rights and artificial intelligence, to name but a few.

Abortion is a highly controversial ethical issue, with a difficult choice to be made between the rights of the unborn fetus versus the rights of the mother. Pro-choice advocates chant that women have the right to control their own bodies, while pro-life advocates scientifically argue that life begins at conception, and that abortion is equivalent to murder.

Euthanasia, also known as assisted suicide, makes headlines too, because of this age-old, open question about free will. Proponents believe that euthanasia can be a humane way to end the suffering of terminally ill individuals, while opponents spiritually (and theologically) promote that the practice goes against the sanctity of life, thus leading to abuse and exploitation.

Genetic engineering is another hot topic that keeps humankind in a quandary. While the process has the potential to cure genetic diseases and improve agricultural output, there are concerns about the ethical implications of manipulating the genetic code of living organisms for irreversible damage.

Climate change is another contentious ethical issue that stems from the enigmatic responsibility of individuals and society, philosophers have alerted the world about. Governments are lobbied to take action and prevent catastrophic environmental damage with renewable energy, spatial planning, sustainable agriculture.

The debate runs between how much we are willing to sacrifice in terms of lifestyle and economic growth to address this global threat (evolutionary change), and the understated technical hindrances to the development of a new environmental order (progress) such as scale feasibility, cost, chasing our tails and the individual right of wilful nonconformity.

Animal rights is a subset of the foregoing global predicament that has gained podium in recent years (moral circle expansion). Ethical considerations include the use of certain "sentient" species in scientific experimentation and food production, as well as the treatment of animals in entertainment venues such as circuses and zoos.

Women's and gender studies of social philosophers have ignited the cultural criticism of modern LGBTQ+ movements and the political activism to solve ethical issues experienced by its community, still subject to attacks and abuse for homophobia, transphobia and biphobia.

Intolerance, aversion and negativity towards homosexual, transsexual or bisexual people (irrational fear, hatred, antipathy and contempt) are nothing more than collateral effects of our social construction of gender.

History wants that man and the male gender represent strength in all its declinations, whereas woman and the female gender (or the Second Sex) personify weakness and its derivatives.

For instance, a gay man who played with dolls in his childhood, dresses pink and engages in anal sex with another man triggers a *gender prejudice*, by proxy rather than based on a characteristic of their own like racism and classism do: dolls and pink are traditionally associated with the feminine sphere, anal sexuality has a higher stigma mainly because a more visible power level play comes into effect (with a dominant and a submissive role) than other sex positions.

Consequently, when a man crosses his "designated" gender role boundary of masculinity, strength, dominance into femininity, weakness, submission, then he is no longer valued as a human being, for the man has become [or is] a woman.

Therefore, homophobia and transphobia are actually by-products of mysoginy, which is in turn gynophoby whitewashing, deeply rooted in the dominant ideology of patriarchy and historical sexism.

Thematic discourses of equal civil rights and gender equality are worked out, in the mainstream, according to the cultural goals of removing dominant constructions of masculinity and femininity, and the primacy of the gendered heterosexual nuclear family (heteronormativity), in order [but not limited] to solve the healthcare and institutional dilemma of discrimination because of sex, gender identity and sexual orientation (e.g. same-sex marriage, transitioning).

The modern movement for LGBTQ+ rights also cast a light on the ethical dilemma of gender identity. Transgender individuals face discrimination and harassment in many aspects of their lives including employment, housing, education and healthcare.

The concept has existed for centuries and has been shaped by political, religious and societal influences. In all cultures, gender identity has been defined by binary gender roles, where men were expected to be masculine and women were meant to be feminine.

In the 20th century, the medical community began to recognize gender as a psychological aspect, other than solely physical.

The term "transgender" was coined during this time to describe individuals who experience a disconnect between their gender identity and biological sex - intersexuality: androgen insensitivity syndrome (AIS) or Morris syndrome.

One of the most prominent ethical positions regarding identity is the right to self-identification. Many reject the notion that gender identity should be determined by biological sex at birth and rather support self-identification for inclusion.

However, the socially-critical stance has led to clashes with medical professionals who believe that gender identity should be based on biological sex, and with those who promulgate religious or cultural beliefs that do not acknowledge the existence of a "third gender" beyond the traditional binary.

The world seems to have accepted the hypothesis that our identity is only subjectively defined. Pronouns play a leading role in the recent campaigns of critical gender theory. Preferred pronouns (such as "he" "she" "they" or self-made alternatives) are increasingly common, at work or in social settings, in order to show respect and recognition for an individual's right to self-identify.

Last but not least, artificial intelligence (AI) is a rapidly developing field and countless ethical questions about the potential risks, and benefits of machines with advanced cognitive abilities sprout like mushrooms. The conversations revolve around problems such as accountability, bias and human discrimination, job displacement, and the relationship between people and machines.

Most argue that the biggest threat to the future making is when AI learned to self-design. AI is a strength too but if we had our act together ethically, it's possible that AI could become a useful servant rather than a tyrannical master - in other words, we shouldn't want to automate it (precautionary principle).

When God knows what we will do tomorrow, it is reasonable to imply that we have no freewill. Theologians nice try to rescue religious credibility by pointing out that free will does imply the divinity who, however omnipotent and omniscient, chose not to use its power to influence the choices of individuals (blessing of life).

Equally, whether there may be morality without God or not is a great unknown. There is no freewill, therefore we should not punish people at all, when people are incapable of taking action and cannot freely choose between good and evil (servant will).

Should we have free will, then ideally we could kill, since each person would have the power to decide the purposes of their actions and determine their own motives including the unscrupulously utilitarian ones (free will as «moral fantasy»).

The actions of each of us that aim to create or modify moral circumstances are denoted by the volitional attitude, or the conscious will to stick to a conduct. This goes as far as even to omit some ethical behaviours and actions to stick to our guns, against all odds.

Despite free will being an unresolved controversy, the matter today has determined strong repercussions in law, where the concept of individual responsibility underpins the codes of civil and criminal procedures.

Governments require all citizens to fulfil the mandatory duties of political, economic and social solidarity.

In a democratic regime, Constitutions clarify that freedom is not intended for free will satisfaction, rather for the realization of common good through full accomplishment of *virtues* and positive collaboration of individuals. More simply, freedom is not free will but only a guideline to be implemented in legislation.

Philippa Foot believed morality has no power on humanity, because people behave morally, only when motivated by other factors.

Social structure and motivation can make morality binding in a sense, but only because it makes moral norms feel inescapable, according to Foot.

It is clear, consequentialism is implausibly demanding and morality seems to affect us only negatively through feelings like shame, pain and ego death.

Evolution invites us to reflect on the fact that *transgression*, more often than not, is a venture for new *possible laws*, leaving behind what is "favoured" as good or right.

### DID YOU KNOW? ▼

Military deception (**ruse de guerre**) is described from ancient to modern times, both in semi-mythical accounts such as the story of the *Trojan Horse* in Virgil's Aeneid and in well-documented events such as the flying of the American flag by the British ocean liner RMS Lusitania in 1915 (whilst the United States was a neutral country) to deter attack by German submarines.

The Air Force's F-117 fighter uses aerodynamics discovered during research into how bumblebees fly.

What separates love, or *eros* from friendship, or *philia* is respectively the evaluative and relational attitude; Aristotle distinguished friendships of pleasure, of utility and of virtue. Nietzsche powerfully synthesised: *"What is a friend? Another myself."*

# CHAPTER VI

# Mind

## *Mental and Physical*

---

Is there more to human cognition than what can be carried out by a computer program?

---

A back-breaking human conundrum is explaining where the mind's ability to represent external reality originates. To put it simply, how can matter (the brain) think and whether an individual "I" really exists or the subject is broken down into a multitude of distinct "cognitive agencies".

From psychology to contemporary neurosciences, philosophies of mind endeavour to answer the long-lasting dilemma with speculative and methodological solutions.

The germinal definition of mind is substance, which is *causa sui* and matter in a materialistic world-view, whose underlying monism would swing between idealism (the matter is an idea) and physicalism (everything is matter) across the ages.

Descartes's *cogito ergo sum* banged to clearly determine the correspondence of our self-evident, distinct mind to reality, overcoming the skeptical doubt that acknowledged thought, but not fully the body.

The line of argument provoked posterity to draw an ontological (there are two distinct substances) and dualistic (mind-body) reflection about human beings, achieved through the use of *cogito*, as the basis of any knowledge. Conclusion argued the knowledge of the mind is primary with respect to that of the body.

The Cartesian critique of matter is placed in a new metaphysical vision that views the universe as constituted by two ontologically opposite substances: matter (*res extensa*) and mind (*res cogitans*).

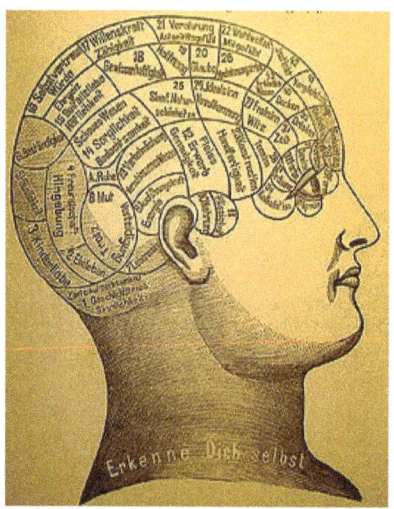

A phrenological mapping of the brain – phrenology was among the first attempts to correlate mental functions with specific parts of the brain although it is now widely discredited.

Crucial to the development of the philosophy of mind is the mystery of the *causal interaction* between mind and body, proposed by Cartesian dualism.

According to the French mathematician, there is a union of two or more elements, between the spiritual ego and the body, which make it one, without a structural correlation (anomalous dualism).

The tie-in shares fundamental 'properties', easily ascribable when sensations such as hunger, thirst, pain present in the mind, certify the existence of our body.

Princess Elizabeth of Bohemia exhorted Descartes to better articulate the causal efficacy of the immaterial mind; in particular, the visible ability of the mind to act on the body.

When she gave the first-person example of how her "condition" of being a woman can influence reason, eureka was that the order of thought does not depend on the causal order of the material or in full inference, that our soul does extend beyond the material (what Chalmers defines nowadays as a *further fact*).

Logical empiricists cast aspersions on the pluralist nature of a unique substance for its inconsistency: the *Principle of Identity* states, in fact, that there are no two separate objects that exactly resemble each other (indiscernibility of identicals), thus two entities with the same properties do not exist (Leibniz's law).

In response, Hobbes argued that thought is only [materialised] objectified language - body with *accidental* mental movement - and for Hume, *reason* is the result of psychological associationism deriving from habit (what later Kahneman dignified as *Bias* in behavioral psychology).

This mechanist and deterministic position fully developed with the concept of causal closure in the physical world, whereby there cannot be non-material causes to physical events, in a material world (Papineau, 1991). Should we dismiss the closure principle, we would have to postulate the independence of mind, explaining clearly why.

Reductive physicalism, in the concrete, defends that

> "The language of the universe is the language of physics and, consequently, all knowledge can be traced back to the statements on physical objects."
>
> CARNAP, 1931

By monist standards, the sleeve trick to solve the paradox of mental causation was to argue that mental events are physical events (type-identity theory): all the mental phenomena always identify with physical causes or neural processes (mind = brain).

However, causal closure excludes that there are mental causes that interfere with physical phenomena and *de facto* appeals to the simplest solution, avoiding unnecessary complications (Okham's Razor).

One can recognize, prima facie, that "there are mental causes of physical events" or more subtly, that "non-physical mental properties (thought, imagination etc.) exist in, or *supervene*, certain physical ones" - in two words, the brain (property dualism).

Davidson's token-type version of the identity theory does not deem possible to describe mental events (nomological or definitional reductionism), despite them being identical with the physical; a mind-body relationship known as "anomalous monism".

In light of this, different revisionist models of Cartesian dualism have been advanced, without completely reducing mind to physics and matter.

Plausible alternative to interactionism is that mental states and physical states do not interact but move in parallel (parallelism).

When objective-oriented behaviorism signalled "the causes on a logical level, starting from their effects" (Watson, 1924), functionalism changed the direction to consider only the functional aspect of the mind and defined mental states as *multiple realizations*, conditional upon their different, causal role (Putnam, 1950).

In Saturday night terms, the mind is a system equivalent to an ideal Turing machine, a continuous macro-processing of inputs and outputs (J. Fodor, *"The Language of Thought"*, 1975), which can now be formulated with a "computable function" - to use a loanword from Alan Turing's model (computational theory of mind).

The *causal exclusion argument* planted by Jaegwon Kim in 1998 grills the hypothesis on the functioning of the mind (functionalism) and justifies a more desirable theory of human cognition.

For functionalism, a mental state is given by its causal position within a series of causes, leading to the accomplishment of a given cognitive task. Kim argues that understanding the nature of mental states, in such wise, embarks two difficult implications: *epiphenomenalism* and *causal overdetermination*.

Epiphenomenalism means that the relationship between mental states would be completely irrelevant to the causal relationship existing between their physical creators; the mind is only an accessory manifestation - an *"epiphenomenon"* - whose presence is not necessary for real phenomena to take place.

Another very counterintuitive effect is that the connections between our conscious thoughts are only apparent: not only does the mind not act on the body, but it does not act on the mind either.

As a result, the implied existence of a mental causality that overlaps physical causality (or *supervenience*) suffices to conclude, jointly and without contradictions, that mental states are not physical states (dualism), they cause certain physical states (interactionism) and they are subject to laws which may explain them completely (materialism).

Kim's *Supervenience argument* and non-reductive physicalism spread the reflection that physical states, although different, are the result of some other properties of the system, understood at a holistic, no longer atomic level.

In other words, they "emerge" as consciousness from the interaction itself, a dominant philosophical position known as *emergentism*.

Today, neurosciences approve that the mind, and therefore thought, emotions and behaviour are just the expression of brain function, being a body part. It is, therefore, plausible to abandon the ontological dualism in favor of a less demanding dualism of properties or functions.

On this wise, mind and body shall be seen as "experiential states" of a polyfunctional organism, as put forward by the most recent genetical research (Bonicelli), rather than a mere processing system, which starts from the human factor to discern physiological from mental states.

# Mind and Experience

---

Can you clearly and distinctly conceive mind existing independently from body?

---

In his *Meditations*, Descartes contended that the mind and the body cannot be the same substance, due to introspection.

Once the position of "inner gaze" is being adopted and we pay attention to the contents of our psychic life (subjective properties of our experience), then, it looks like indubitable that *qualia* are, in no way, the same as the objects of the physical world.

A very similar reflection characterized Sophists' idea that reality is appearance (everything is in our mind), shaped Schopenhauer's concept of tainted will and fast forward, the rise of phenomenism: the impossibility to know the ["thing in itself"] substance, as being transcendental, with no ontological reality (noumenon).

For the late philosopher and psychologist Daniel Dennett, the ability to explain life without resorting to transcendental entities or principles gives Darwinian theory - one of the naturalistic theses, *par excellence* - its strength and validity.

Accepting the boxing match, Searle's philosophical goal was to show how the mind is a biological phenomenon, like photosynthesis or digestion and how such, while being irreducible to brain states, has specific and important causal relationships with them (biological naturalism).

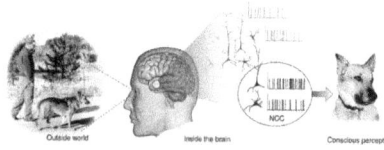

*Schema of the neural processes underlying consciousness, from Christof Koch*

Regrettably, bringing all of reality back to the natural [empirically observable] datum and appraise that as "knowable" only through the method of natural sciences is grinding. The explanation of a fact, especially on a moral level, does not constitute its justification.

Paradoxically postulated, even a cat closed in a box could be alive and dead, at the same time, until the box is opened and an observation is made (Schroedinger's cat, 1935). That is, interactionism is hard to murder.

For the avoidance of doubt, philosopher Joseph Levine, before others, accounted how physical and conscious experience would always have an *explanatory gap;* for instance, defining pain in physiological terms is elusive.

Naturalists like Dennett, in faith, admitted that scientific models are only tools that allow us to conveniently conceive phenomena and, possibly, to anticipate them through predictions (instrumentalism). Nonetheless, the philosopher also presented instances of our subjective, conscious experience, what [quality] we feel but we cannot describe in words.

*Qualia* have four fundamental characteristics: they are ineffable, therefore it is not possible by definition to transmit them in words; they are intrinsic, that is, simple elements that cannot be traced back to others; they are private, not comparable to those of other subjects; and they are directly apprehensible, that is immediate and therefore, not influenced by consciousness.

In a nutshell, it is no longer possible to base the search for good, evil or knowledge only on experience, as this cannot absolutely constitute an objective criterion.

One of the first philosophers to counteroffer an interesting response to this, without defining *qualia* was the 17-century Frenchman Blaise Pascal. The French philosopher argued that we know things automatically in two distinct ways: the "geometric spirit" (rational) and the "spirit of refinement" (our subjective experience).

To better understand the concept, it is useful to mention the *inverted spectrum argument*, first proposed by John Locke. Let's imagine that two people see a strawberry: the first perceives it as red but the other as green (*qualia*).

Both people will say that the strawberry is red, regardless, for they have learned to use a language, so their own personal *"quale"* (the experience of strawberry colour) relates to the concept of "red". Due to the ineffability of qualia, the fruit represents two different sensations on a subjective level (what-is-like for them).

It follows that, in any case, the hunt for truth (agreeing on the strawberry colour) remains objective, while disconnected from subjective knowledge.

To further understand how knowledge of a phenomenon may disconnect from the perceptual sphere - how mind can be distinct from body - we shall examine Frank Johnson's thesis from his hero paper *"What Mary Did Not Know"* (1986).

The thought experiment imagined a woman who grew up all her life in a room without windows, without mirrors, in a position to be able to see, only and exclusively, black and white. However, Mary is passionate about neurosurgery and can access a manual concerning the perception of colours by the brain. By studying, Mary might get to know perfectly what it means to see a colour, to ensure no ignorance on the topic.

Yet, if one day, Mary could get out of the room and really see the colours, she would undoubtedly learn something new, despite knowing everything on the topic.

This is not just an epistemic paradox. Mary would simply acquire new *qualia* linked to new experiences, meaning that the experience serves to know, mainly what is unrelated to truth - Mary rationally knew everything she would never apply to the experience.

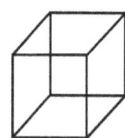 

The Necker cube and Rubin vase can be perceived in more than one way.

By reasoning like this, experience acquires an inestimable and ontologically necessary value, no longer just as a theoretically useful and nomologically superfluous verification tool.

Experience is not epistemologically essential but Jackson's knowledge argument excludes why thought depends on external features (that is, qualia are epiphenomenal).

Paul Churchland later sustained the necessity of knowing the *qualia*, by providing neurological evidence about brain exposure to light and visual development. In his own words:

> "Learning transmits information, but experiencing communicates abilities."

WHAT EXPERIENCE TEACHES, LEWIS, D.K., 2004

Many disprove the existence of *qualia* altogether, contending there is no "veil of perception" and the "qualitative aspects of experience" are an incoherent concept (Michael Tye); plus, they find impossible for one to have a dialogue with oneself (*Private Language Argument*, Wittgenstein, 1953).

Others suspect that one shall not identify *qualia* with their objective sources to reify them (Moreland, 1983) and that neurobiological models are going to eventually map the mechanism creating them (Orpwood, 2007).

The personal character of experience makes it very difficult to conceive mind existing independently from body and account for this "subjective, intrinsic, what-its-like-ness" (Nagel, 1979).

The dilemma is now known as the *hard problem of consciousness* and should we all have a physically analogous look-alike, without soul, we wouldn't be able to tell the difference about its lack of *sentience* (P-Zombie Argument).

A fortiori, conceivability implies, without fail, metaphysical possibility (Chalmers, 1996), therefore, "mental states supervene naturally and they are ontologically distinct".

## *On Consciousness*

---

Does consciousness create reality?
Is the possession of intentionality what distinguishes the mental from the non-mental?

---

In the last thirty years, there have established three main interdisciplinary positions on the concept of mind, still in competition:

1. the **study of the "mental"**, other than the mind pervaded by its own properties;
2. the **mind as a product or activity of the brain** from a strictly medical-scientific viewpoint;
3. the **mind as a computational machine**, a theory lately in vogue, for its role in AI (artificial intelligence) and robotics.

At the intersection of monist and dualist factions, Popper interposed a plural vision: three worlds that, in essence, are only one - the only possible and liveable one.

World 1 includes physical bodies, World 2 is the mental or psychological one (pleasure and pain, thoughts and perceptions), World 3 features the products of the human mind. In a critically realist vein, the philosopher admitted the reality of mental states, because they interact with our body.

His anti-reductionist theory has fuelled three major strands in this multi-disciplinary inquiry:

- the Mind-Body problem
- the Mind-World problem
- the Mind-Mind problem

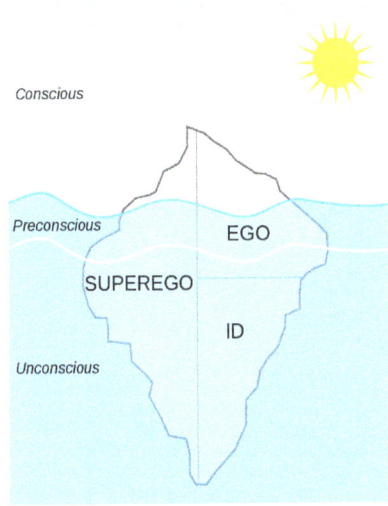

An iceberg is often used to provide a visual representation of Freud's theory that most of the human mind operates unconsciously.

Any of these relations builds upon the existence of a character resulting from the active and wilful participation of our consciousness in a given experience: *intentionality*.

The term stands for the reference of all psychic acts to an objective correlate: that is, the "constitutive attitude of thought to always have a content and continually be directed to an object".

With Brentano, intentionality is what separates the psychic phenomena from the physical ones.

For its metaphysical characteristic, Husserl further defines it as *trascendental*, that is, consciousness is intentional.

Depending on the context where it is observed, consciousness is generally understood in the following ways: as a state or act of being conscious, as opposed to the unconscious (subjective experience of events or sensations), as a state of alertness of the mind as opposed to coma, plus as moral and spiritual awareness.

Introspection is placed at the core of the conscious path, as "subjective awareness of oneself" leading to solipsism (*consciousness*), which is acknowledged only in the intention (as a Hegelian spirit), with the awareness of the external world (*self-consciousness*).

On the sleeve of this thesis, every experience is stamped by the negating action of conscience, which grows precisely by opposing the "being of things" and giving life, to *non-being*: "The Being through which Nothing comes into the world" (Sartre, *Being and Nothingness*, 1956).

The question of intentionality incidentally resolved at linguistic level, since language cannot help but turn to statements of belief or statements of propositional attitudes, in general (Chisholm).

For Searle, when the living organism relates to the world, its brain / mind necessarily disposes itself, in certain *"intentional states"*, which can be labeled as action, belief, desire, expectation, etc. As an explanatory model of intentional states, the American philosopher used his theory of "speech acts".

That being said, the set of phenomena that go by the name of intentionality is essentially functional to an interpretative practice - the *intentional stance,* the intentional attitude operating in the psychology of common sense - based on beliefs, desires and intentions (Dennett), thus equally applicable to any biological system (human and animal) including technological ones.

In line with this helpful gloss on the issue, propositional attitudes were formally not taken as truth-bearer. Their meaning has no truth-value (denotation), rather is just a connotation - the psychological charge associated with the term (Frege).

One of the giants among twentieth-century philosophers, Carnap further exemplified the distinction by introducing the case of *Possible Worlds*.

"The *intension* of a concept is its definition" (or understanding) while the *extension* is "its range of applicability" (or reference); that is, meaning is *mediated* by description (Quine's *"myth of meaning"*) and is fundamentally a behavioural accident.

These reflections have attributed to the notion of intentionality a central role in the theory of consciousness.

For starters, Kant's reviewed theory, where morality is understood as the *"voice of conscience"*. By conceiving intentionality, as strictly connected to the cultural dimension - and whereby people develop psychological characteristics - made it possible to define consciousness, not only in "natural" but also in "cultural" terms.

This is what J. Margolis recommended by defining intentionality, in terms of precise social practices and certain cultural institutions that govern human conduct.

In the wake of such consideration, consciousness became awareness that a subject has of oneself, and of the external world which has a relationship with; therefore, also an awareness of its own identity (the conception that one has of oneself, within the individual and society), not only of the whole of one's inner activities.

In artificial intelligence and cognitive sciences, this philosophical ferment inaugurated a controversial subject, because intentionality, in these denominations, is taken as something that a machine could never *really* possess, from a structural standpoint.

Therefore, for Searle and other philosophers, it makes no sense to assimilate the mind (or consciousness) to a computer, as no computer can "think" with the same depth, as human beings (*Chinese Room Argument*).

Spiritualism, from Maine de Biran's to Bergson's introspectionism, has regarded consciousness a privileged access to self-knowledge, therefore the foundation of any speculation.

This designation of consciousness has increasingly accentuated its immanent traits, with an emphasis on the psychological aspect as *"stream of lived experiences"*, thus consolidating an absolute subjectivity (or a *transcendental* ego).

With research progress on brain functions and the development of Freud's psychoanalytic theories on its limit, consciousness earned the main stage of experimental investigations.

Studies of psychology and neurosciences have extended the notion of the *unconscious*, from the psychodynamic sphere to the sphere of cognitive processes (*cognitive unconscious*).

They have expanded the idea of consciousness, from "indistinct flow of thoughts and emotions" to an "integrated system of operations, partly conscious and partly unconscious".

Scientific revolution carried out by neurosciences had long ignored emotions, as if they were not part of the mind and brain.

In his decades-long investigations, Jaak Panksepp set out to make up for this lack, scientifically proving that "emotional affects are not intentional, they are not propositional attitudes and they do not require language" (*Affective Neuroscience*, 1998; *Archeology of the Mind*, 2012).

Propositional attitudes are therefore, eliminable by the most developed neuroscience.

## DID YOU KNOW? ▼

Hypocrites was the first to make a systematic categorisation of diseases and its treatments, using prognosis and clinical observation - the basics of clinical medicine, as it is practiced today - and established medicine as a discipline distinct from magic (**theurgy**) or natural philosophy. Critics of evidence-based medicine have raised numerous questions regarding the unreliability of mechanistic, medical research, most notably clinical trials, the hierarchy of evidence used or placebo.

When you have a toothache, the pain is in your highly malleable brain, not in your mouth: neurosciences discovered how we cannot feel pain, without a brain and the nerves sending signals to our mind - **anaesthesia** reversibly causes *"unconsciousness"* all while dreaming and sleep, since 1804.

The *cup-and-balls illusion* is 2000 years old, performed by ancient Roman conjurers and igniting the focus on dexterity of magicians. History's most famous illusionist Jean Robert Houdin helped legitimize stage magic as an art form with mentalism and using physics for escapology tricks. Illusionistic tradition in art history capitalises on introspection, our genuine attempt to misrepresent experiences (optical illusions or anamorphosis).

# CHAPTER VII

# Metaphysics

## *On Being and Existence*

---

Do the following statements have the same logical form:
*"George Washington is President"* and *"George Washington exists"*?

---

Reality is intrinsically linked to ontology, that is, to the philosophical discipline that deals with what exists. Metaphysics is the science of absolute reality that gives the third degree to the deep structures and ultimate causes of the world - everything that goes beyond (*metà*) the senses or physics (*physis*).

With Aristotle, metaphysics incarnated the first philosophy or theory of *"being as being"*, screening the primary principles of reality as qualities, rather than its natural (physical) or logical-quantitative (mathematical) features. The ultimate goal here is the truth itself, necessary for every other science.

Prerequisite of metaphysics is the research on the limits and possibilities of a knowledge that *transcends* - which exists outside of sensible reality (e.g. the other, the triangle, nature) or above (e.g. God, our Ego). This provides metaphysics a powerful epistemological thrust, as we do not know what we know yet, nor what is truth.

Metaphysical philosophers championed that there could be no actual knowledge, unless such does arise from intelligence, because experience is deceptive: it has particular things as its object, science instead has universals as its object, and these are, notably, in the very soul of things.

Intuition or the "perception of perception" (*apperception*, from Leibniz), in the act of thought, is the origin and goal of all metaphysics, since the subject is immediately identical to the object (consciousness). In contrast, logic (or reason) is only an analytical tool to communicate the intuitive vision of the universal, and therefore, knowledge is mediated.

Gustave Courbet - Le Desespere, 1845

Philosophers have often defined existence in the negative: an object is real, if it is not simply the fruit of someone's imagination, that such is part of the present as a material reality (principle of individuation) distinct by its essence - «which whereby a certain thing is what it is, and not another thing»- (Aristotle) - and *causa sui*, different from the subject (i.e. substance).

The Aristotelian concept of substance as matter, *horror vacui*, and beyond any change or becoming (as opposed to the accidental) diverted to a misrepresentation of the ontological reality of objects, "postulating a substratum for all that is revealed in experience". Notable examples include Kant, who denied substance any ontological reality and reduced it to a completely subjectivated, transcendental activity up to the inconsistent, scientific debate, before the advent of Einstein.

The verb "to be" (to exist) is commonly used as existence, identity or predication.

To be honest, a terminological distinction between being and existence is due: while being is "in itself" and *per se,* and does not need anything else, existence does not have "being" in its own right; instead, it receives that from something else (*ex* means out of).

Being is something absolute, while existence is always subordinated to a higher being, on which it depends. Such tension toward the absolute [God] and transcendence has been the driving force of other metaphysical disciplines (e.g. psychology, cosmology, theology) subsumed under "special metaphysics".

Sisyphus, the symbol of the absurdity of existence, painting by Franz Stuck (1920)

Ontologists interrogate if it is possible, and in what terms, to attribute existence to abstract entities (e.g., love, fear), properties (red, beautiful, hot, etc.), propositions (George Washington is President), transcendent and fantastic entities (God, hell, unicorns), actions or events (the walk, the football match), social structures (money, government) as well as mathematical objects (numbers, sets, operators).

Linguists object to that because there is already an understanding among those who use abstract concepts, so it is difficult to argue that these do not exist.

After the "linguistic turn", philosophers no longer aim to know whether roses or tables exist - for no one doubts this - but what makes roses and tables, in reality, roses and tables.

Being George Washington is, therefore, the infinitive of "is" and it is precisely in the indicative form that it is frequently rendered, which highlights its actual nature: being, the type of being that an individual possesses (or citing Heidegger, *Dasein*) "happens" (*Geschiet*).

The German philosopher empowered that "being manifests itself precisely through the word, and in particular through language" or beautifully put it:

"Language is the house of being."

Despite philosophical contributions like this to ontology and phenomenology, the "physical" or independent existence of an object is yet to have its finest definition, battered by the intuitive, physicalist notion of "space stably occupied in time" or the reductionist use of *properties* - W.V. Quine widely attacked - that identify matter by weight, shape and state.

Frege and Russell observed that "to be" is not a predicate of logic or, accurately, it is not a first-order predicate; the implication is that existence is not a property that can be attributed to an object or be identified with. Miller offered a formal demonstration of how existence is configured as a predicate: a property (being President) implies existence (being), with no need to quantify it - $\exists$ logically formalizes the existence that *"there exists at least one x satisfying the predicate P"*.

Since the Middle Ages, the dispute over universals sought to fix the problem: the identity and existence of ideal (or fictitious, immaterial, imaginary) entities instead of concrete (or empirical/sensitive, materials, real) ones.

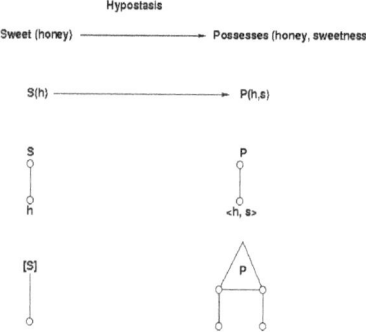

The transformation of "honey is sweet" into "honey possesses sweetness" can be viewed in several ways.

The anomaly is whether universals (humanity, the dog, the storm, red, existence and being President) have an ontological consistency typical of the real (realist position) or they are only descriptive words representing general concepts (that is, semantic categories not endowed with the property of existence), which are used when we are not talking about specific space-time instances (nominalist position).

As a result, we are left with two emergency exits here: (1) we value *"is President"* and *"exists"* as logically identical (in the form A=B), for both are just descriptive concepts (universals) showing similarity of attribute (predicative nominalism) and thus, no correspondance to reality is required; or (2) we take both statements as logically correct but *real* (true), pending ontological validity and this begs the question.

Besides monism (e.g. Leibzin, *one substance*) and dualism (e.g. Descartes, *mind-body*), reality is articulated further, after John Locke distinguished it into primary (independent properties of objects) and secondary (dependent properties of objects) qualities, strongly influencing the psychological theory whereby the mind (or idealism) has more leverage in *persisting* (identity) and standing out as characteristic and unique, compared to the body (realism).

The physicalist approach to metaphysics is driven by the defenders of the dogma that "everything is physical" and logical properties may also be demonstrated, with the universal language of physics (e.i. Canberra Plan).

Nevertheless, naturalistic analyses of the sort progressively prove insufficient and inconsistent to effectively pick out features of our cognitive behavior in the world (e.g., neuroplasticity, vagueness).

Some philosophers like J. Mackie endorsed the Lockean view that some qualities are secondary, in the sense that they never really exist in bodies, except as powers.

For those who think (create), reality has no mysteries. The underlying notion of reality is a creative process attributable to the Absolute, going to transform the immutability characteristic of identity into a "dynamic" concept (Schelling, Hegel).

For Bergson, "existence is the victory over nothing", while the *non-being*, according to logic, is not, by its very definition.

Perhaps the priority of humankind shall be understanding thoroughly the idea of *nothing*, in order to define the borders and limits of *being*.

# *The Order of Time*

---
### Does time have a beginning or an end?
---

As we live and age, we relentlessly become aware time goes by and how helpless we are, with respect to its order.

"Time passing" stamps the phenomena, material and spatial changes of our experience but is said to be nothing more than a projection of our *consciousness*.

The concept of time does not find a univocal correspondence in physics, where it is not possible to absolutely sequence the apparent succession of events, as they happen by human observation, other than minimally. Yet, everything that moves in space or transfigures within is described by the human mind, on a temporal level.

Philosophers examined the time in various ways, throughout the history - Zeno's paradoxes, for instance, defiantly challenged the primordial concept with the impossibility of motion but the definitions of Plato, and Aristotle, have been the reference for many centuries, right up until the scientific revolution.

Plato conceived time as "the moving image of eternity", whereas Aristotle branded it to be the measure of movement, with "before" and "after", thus space is strictly necessary to define time.

For Augustine, time was a subjective entity. According to Newton, time (like space) is *"sentium Dei"* (sense of God) and flows immutable, always the same as itself - a similar concept is present in the works of Galileo Galilei.

Worthy of note is the quarrel between Newton and Leibniz on the question of absolute time. The former believed that time was, like space, a container of events, the latter believed that time, like space, was a conceptual apparatus describing the interrelationships between the events themselves.

Einstein radically changed the notion of *simultaneity* (two events can coincide for one observer, but not for another).

According to his relativity theory, the measurement of time intervals is not absolute but relative to the observer, and only the speed of light is the same for all the observers.

Solving the paradox of twins, who travel and age at different times, we observe the phenomenon of the so-called *"time dilation"*. Consequently, another way of naming the order of time can be that of a simple "change of state," therefore also closely linked to the dimension of "space" - concerning the observer(s) of the phenomenon itself (a plastic dimension, called *spacetime*).

Another significant contribution of this genre to the perception of time is obtained by Henri Bergson, who observed how the time of physics does not coincide with that of consciousness. As a measurement of physical phenomena, in fact, time is resolved in a *spatialization* (such as the hands of the clock), wherein each instant is objectively represented and qualitatively identical to all the others (*chrònos*); the original time is found in our consciousness, which knows the former through intuition - it is subjective, and each instant is qualitatively different from all the others (*kairos* or late Jung's *synchronicity*).

The human perception of "time" is the projection that consciousness constructs so that the reality we are a part of, is materially modified.

Temporal illusions succeeded in exposing the neural mechanisms underlying such distorted perception of time. A prime of this is *chronostasis*, an illusion that seems to make an image that precedes a rapid eye movement last longer than actually happened. Presentism views the past and the future as human-mind interpretations of movement, instead of real parts of time (or dimensions), which coexist with the present.

As a more intuitive reference, matter "is", and (at the same time) "becomes" (that is, it assumes another form).

The obviousness of this assertion is often misleading: the statement underlies a contradiction, for the being of an object is certified by its identity (over time), or by its permanent existence (persistence); becoming, on the other hand, presupposes transformation, that is the diversity (of the form), for which it imposes a "before" and an "after", that is to say, an [interval of] "time" which scientifically, instead, carries no explanation.

The Persistence of Memory, Salvador Dalí, 1931
One of the most recognizable paintings of Surrealism on time.

In Western philosophy, time always originates from transformation. The controversy between temporalists and atemporalists, which distinguishes the analytic philosophy of time, spread around the notion of change.

Temporal becoming means a change that concerns the events and also the instants (its units): it is about moving from being future to being present and from being present to being future.

Therefore, it is impossible for perfectly identical individual objects to exist, having all their properties in common (Leibniz's *identity of indiscernibles*).

Since Bergson, time assumed the new meaning of "duration".

One way of defining the concept of "after" is based on the assumption of apparent *causality* to human experience. Humankind's work, such as creating and improving calendars, and clocks, increased understanding of the evident nature of time (eternalism) and its relative measurement (past, present, future).

Hume exhibits the critique of the *cause-effect* principle, or the possibility of other worlds (counterfactual theory), considered infallible by the scientific mentality. Every belief, he points out, derives from "a habit that gives rise to a view that is, therefore, irrational, instinctual, and not necessarily certain".

However, in the history of philosophy, humanity's action has been constantly conceived as *consciously* directed to the achievement of goals through time. Few philosophers, such as Thomas Hobbes and Baruch Spinoza, have instead rated that conception of human action irrelevant or erroneous (contingency) and have developed a deterministic doctrine (necessity).

The self-portrait The Two Fridas is one of the most notable and recognized Kahlo's works, depicting two versions of herself seated together: her pain during her divorce and the subsequent transitioning of her novel identity.

As a result, the main orders of time are linear and circular. In the cyclical concept, events repeat themselves (samsara) in an ongoing circle (Kalpa), where free will exists only as Sisyphus's surrender to the absurd (incompatibilism). For the linear concept, human history has a predetermined meaning, but it arises from the purely religious idea (fatalism) and to reach a goal (teleology); in this case, free will, in good and evil, is decisive (compatibilism).

Time is, for most philosophers, just a mental abstraction and time tracking is superfluous.

They do not seem to be entirely wrong because the past is no longer, the future is not yet, the present as a separation between past and future - two things that do not exist - cannot exist, consequently. And if I clapped my hands in your face, you might say that the noise you heard really *just* happened, yet, by the time you think about it, the noise has already happened; the noise has passed. You could obviously stop my hands, before my next clap and argue that I am going to make the noise now but what you may actually mean is that I will do it - in the future - albeit imminent.

John Ellis McTaggart believed, for his part, that time and change were mere illusions (idealism) and the becoming of time is impossible. The English philosopher makes use of an essential distinction between the "A series" order (dynamic, continuously subject to change) and the "B series" stack (static, the relations that constitute it are immutable).

The first consists of the series of moments (or their "contents"), that is, the events ordered by what will then be called *"properties A"*; their being present, past or future. On the other hand, the second is a series of moments or events ordered by the so-called *"B relations"*, such as simultaneity and temporal precedence.

While modern physics believe that time is as *real* as space, atemporalist positions like MacTaggart's favour the *unreality of time*, considered as a consequence of self-contradiction - being its *flow* both present and not present.

As a result, any description of *becoming* incurs a thunderstorm. One of the most original and recent contributions to the concept of order of time as "changing" is that of the philosopher Emanuele Severino (2020): everything that has the property of *being* has, by the very nature of being, the property of *being eternal*. Therefore, what is, must have been and will be. Change as a form of identity (or *persistence*) is still widely accepted as plausible. And iffy.

### DID YOU KNOW?

Animals use Earth's magnetic field to know their location and ants take rest for around 8 Minutes, in 12-hour period.

In 1848, Nobel scientist William Crookes was the first to confirm the possibility of physical contact with the spirit world, reporting the Fox sisters' ability to converse with deceased entities and the materializations of Katie King's spirit by the medium Florence Cook. Joseph Banks Rhine devised the method of the Zener Cards and provided rich documentations of the existence of clairvoyance, psychokinesis or ESP - Extrasensory Perception, just like the Ganzfeld experiments often claim evidence of telepathy.

We believe in electrons and blackholes, even if we can't see them.

# CHAPTER VIII

# Science

## *Evidence, Thinking and Scientific Truth*

> Do we have any reason to believe that what has happened regularly, in the past, will continue to happen?

The powerful criticism broached by David Hume on the validity of induction, during the 18th century, elevated philosophical aspects that since antiquity and up until then, were underground scholarship.

A modern and better structured explanation of the "problem of induction" crystallized into the impossibility of demonstrating the correctness of universally valid laws, obtained by generalizing the observational results of a finite, number of cases.

Aristotle first told the world about differences of cognitive modalities, yet always underestimated the role of induction, which always *necessarily* needed empirical practice.

In his concept of *episteme* or science, there was no such component: it was rather a contemplative vision (epagoghé). Induction gained power with Galileo Galilei and Francis Bacon, when the new [Galilean] science became *empiria*, that is, experience.

Galilei's catch phrase *"knowledge is the daughter of experience"* signifies that if there is no experience, it is not possible to draw rules, laws or theories in the scientific field.

In *Sidereus Nuncius* (1610), Galileo explicited several discoveries made from his observations with the telescope. On account of some observations, he formulated general rules of astronomical and physical nature; Galilei is a theorist of *inductive inference*, father of the logic of scientific discovery.

A famed statesman Francis Bacon also sought to enhance induction, attacking Galileo's theories which, according to him, did not have a systematic work on the observation of individual cases.

The English philosopher then introduced the "*tabula absentiae et presentiae*", laboratory tools that allow the scientist to include or exclude elements, with respect to the observations made. Crystal clear, a framework to experiment cause and effects, in order to infer a scientific theory in a more valid, necessary and certain way.

Bacon's overconfidence in inductive inference, which could lead to absolutely certain truths, gathered the criticisms of many later philosophers of science, prominently David Hume. The latter reflected on the possibilities of proving inductive conclusions, through the *principle of uniformity*.

In his opinion, induction can never be justified. In reality, everything we conclude in the past or in the present cannot predict the future. People can observe innumerable possible cases of a certain series of objects or events, yet the future is never certain. Therefore, we cannot assume that in the future, events will be the same way.

At the core of induction, there is the mechanism of its incompleteness. Induction makes sense, if we look at a certain number of cases and generalize, for all possible cases. But the strength is also a weakness: to generalize all cases too is to *probably* generalize an error; the next observation or experiment may not be the same as those made before.

In the opinion of Hume, "the possible is never false, *a priori*", there is no certainty that is possible to conceive of changes over time - nature may not always be regular.

Given induction does not have an absolute consistency in its certainty and science is founded on an inductive basis, Hume's assessment of induction knocked the bottom out of the validity of modern, experimental science.

Amongst others in the history of science, Bertrand Russell noted the weakness of inductive thinking, with a legendary, metaphorical witticism: also a turkey being fed everyday would be induced to believe tomorrow, it would be fed again, as today happened, yet "tomorrow" is Thanksgiving Day and the only one to eat will be his farmer.

One more case for the limitations of the inductive-logic method was put forward by Carl Gustav Hempel (1945), with his paradox of the ravens.

Its formulation set out to devalue the theory of confirmability, whereby "the acquisition of a new empirical confirmation of a theory increases the probability that this theory is true". Hempel began with the observation that the logical proposition "all crows are black" is logically equivalent to "all non-black objects are not crows".

The paradoxical conclusion does it, because common sense tends to reject the option that a red apple can support the crows thesis and since non-black objects are enormously greater than the number of crows, the real contribution it can make is infinitesimal.

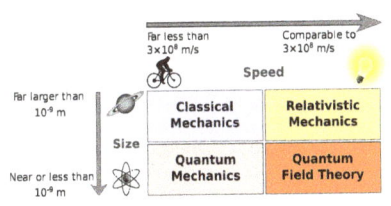

The basic domains of physics

The criterion of evidence as a sign of truth (or scientific proof) is the bedrock of the criticism and consequent development of numerous theories on the scientific method.

The theory of probability and statistics have respectively become the basis and the instrument of the scientific method, while remaining deeply ambiguous.

In probability, a phenomenon is considered observable exclusively from the stand of the possibility or otherwise of its occurrence, regardless of its nature.

Due to this, statistical inference induces generalizations by particular, random observations (sample), that is, an estimate of confirmation, an *inference to the best explanation* (likelihood). Under this method, we have sufficient reason to believe that what has happened regularly in the past will continue to happen.

Bayesian inference is an approach to statistical inference: probabilities are not interpreted as similar frequencies, proportions or concepts (classical probability), but rather as levels of confidence in the occurrence of a given event (subjective).

All in all, there are clear difficulties in using probability as a theory of confirmation and evidence; the error usually consists in correctly identifying the events (Bertrand's box paradox), in not distinguishing different events (the Boy or Girl paradox), in not accepting that a new, acquired information changes the probability itself (Monty Hall problem) and most importantly, in assuming (wrongly) that the fact that an event has probability 1 implies that, it always happens (rather than almost surely).

Induction went into full crisis with the falsificationism of the philosopher Karl Popper (1902-1994). No matter how high the number of favourable cases is, induction cannot predict whether the subsequent one will also be, because the method of reasoning proceeds *a posteriori*. In view of this, Popper exposed how induction cannot be used to justify universal laws formulated *a priori*, while falsification only requires a counter-example to invalidate a theory.

Falsificationism, as opposed to verificationism, claims that the main activity of a researcher is to invalidate a theory by observation or experiment. The advantage of Popper's idea is that truths can be falsified when more knowledge and resources are available.

Even long accepted philosophies such as gravity, relativity and evolution are steadily more challenged, and adapted.

One of the drawbacks of falsificationism is the relationship between theory and observation. Thomas Kuhn, among others, argued that observation is itself strongly theory-laden, in the sense that what one observes is often significantly affected by one's previously held theoretical beliefs.

For Popper, theory always precedes observation: even in any alleged "empirical" and "inductive" approach, the human mind unconsciously tends to superimpose its own mental schemes on the observed reality. What is often passed off as "induction" is, in the concrete, a deduction, for it is always constructed *a priori*; induction is only its negative limit, and fit the bill not to build but to demolish.

*The astronaut Bruce McCandless and Earth are both in free fall.*

Popper, thus, replaced the idea of a *science* based on pure routine of enumeration, with the concept of science made of daring conjectures and a continuous search for *error*, in view of the truth, which remains its regulative ideal.

In the contemporary epistemological debate on induction, the reflection of mereologist Nelson Goodman fills the gap: scientific knowledge does not consist in passive observation, rather in constructive activity.

Such is expressed by the writing of a schematic and selective map of reality, obtained by induction.

Effective practice, like it has historically developed, corroborates the value of a hypothesis. The validity of induction is therefore not formed on its logical validity (as Aristotle argued), nor on its conformity to the nature of the human mind (as David Hume argued), rather on common truth - as Socrates, the founder of inductivism firstly maintained.

Its justifiability or sustainability shapes over time, so as to answer the diffidence posed by a specific human community.

> "The oldest and strongest emotion of mankind is fear, and the oldest and strongest kind of fear is fear of the unknown."
>
> **H. P. LOVECRAFT,** *SUPERNATURAL HORROR IN LITERATURE*

Even now, why we yawn, laugh or age is obscure.

# Mystery, Pseudosciences and the Problem of Demarcation

---

There is no useful distinction between science and non-science.

---

The problem of demarcation bulks large in philosophical discussions on scientific inquiry in order to draw the limits of science, out of the inability to clearly tell the latter from pseudosciences and because metaphysical strands made the whole matter increasingly moot.

Demarcation is pragmatically resolved, in the field of law, with the distinction between theories acceptable by a jury - as an evidential element - and those that are not acceptable.

The Alchemist in Search of the Philosopher's Stone, by Joseph Wright, 1771

In the United States, the confines were defined in 1923 with the sentence *Frye v. US*. The case of murder established the principle, whereby "the data the deduction is based on must have reached such a *consensus judgment*, as to be generally accepted in the specific scientific field". This is now referred to as the *Frye's test*.

Since then, the borderline between science and pseudoscience formalized a certain dependence of jurisprudence on the scientific community, and on its decisions. The defendant's request to use the lie detector to prove their innocence, was abandoned.

In 1993, another ruling reversed the situation, denying the obligation of judges to refer to statements of the scientific community. Those who preside over court proceedings are left with the responsibility of verifying the scientific relevance and reliability of the case evidence: to choose and determine officially which theories and hypotheses conform to the scientific method.

This is the product of *Daubert v. Merrel Dow Farmaceutical Inc.* trial verdict, which delineated the criteria for the scientific reliability of the tests and therefore, practically, for the degree of separation.

One of the central Enlightenment thinkers, Kant can be labeled as a precursor to the the demarcation problem, with his legendary criticism.

In the course of history, conjectures formerly considered scientific and legit by all, were consequently enclosed in the realm of pseudo-sciences (e.g. astrology, alchemy, phrenology and physiognomy).

Pseudoscientific disciplines claim to be based on presumably real, proven facts and events, even if occasionally those are only conditional on the sensations, impressions and desires of the "researchers" who deal with them.

Pseudosciences are defined as "pseudo", not for what they research about, but for the way in which they research that; for the lack of adherence to *reproducibility* and *intersubjective verifiability*, typical of science.

Off the top of my head, parapsychology has always offered honest research, prepared and hell-bent on to apply the scientific method to their chosen field of inquiry. However, in the province of pseudo-sciences when a rigorous scientific method is applied, as in the case of those researchers, significant results are hardly ever obtained.

The contrasting parallel between science and faith has greatly contributed to the contestation on the boundaries between what is science and what is not. A symbol is evolution, sponsored by Charles Darwin in his famous *The origin of species*, in 1859. The theory was opposed to the Church's idea of creationism; and it is still somewhat dominating.

"God of the gaps" is a theological perspective where gaps in scientific knowledge are taken to be evidence or proof of God's existence. Once science was separated from religion, however, the controversy upgraded to what separates these two domains.

*The astrological signs of the zodiac*

The first academics to sustain the argument were the members of the Vienna circle (exponents of logical positivism), who put a name to two fundamental phases in the process of forming scientific knowledge: discovery and justification.

While the first occurs by intuition, the second stage involves logical analysis on the relations between the experimental data and the hypothesis on the agenda.

The Vienna circle discerned between analytical (a priori) and synthetic (empirical) statements, with knowledge being considered scientific, only if it uses synthetic ones (e.g. physics). Moreover, the unique feature of science, from other types of knowledge, was the verification phase.

Hanging out with these philosophers, the problem of demarcation settles in the pursuit of the sufficient and necessary condition that gives the value of "truth" to an affirmation, those sentences that had an empirical meaning - a principle called verificationism.

Karl Popper pointed to the criterion of falsifiability as a means of marking science off what is not. It is necessary to remember that, to have the certainty of the truth of a statement, infinite observations would be necessary. This happens because, to prove its universal validity, infinite verifications are obligatory.

Proportionately, it is easier and safer to make an observation contrary to the theory set out which, in fact, falsifies it. What signalizes a scientific theory, for Popper, is therefore its ability to predict future phenomena and the possibility of being disproved by an observation (or experience) that refutes it.

Scientific theories can only be evidenced through rigorous experimentation, by the book. This is not the case in general, though.

The statement "Botticelli's *Birth of Venus* is stunning", for starters, is an unfalsifiable hypothesis, because there is no experiment that might show this statement to be false.

Parallax method and equations conventionally determined that the average distance between the Earth and the Moon is 384 400 km (238 855 miles). Now, if we were to conduct hands-on investigation for its validation or an audit to demonstrate its falsification, direct testing of such a distance measure would require a scientist to physically travel the space, with a giant ruler to calculate the scale between the two points.

By attacking induction, philosophers roused the gullible minds on how scientific theories are abstract in nature. To cite another example, the answer to the famous question *"How Long Is the Coast of Britain"* is highly dependent on the choice of cartographic scales: different scales or resolutions may result in different observations, and hence opposite conclusions - in fact, this problem is called "scale effect" or scale dependency, in geography.

Calculating the distance between geographical coordinates, in terms of latitude and longitude is always based on some level of abstraction and expressing distances in the astronomical unit allowed scientists to overcome the difficulty of defining distances in fanciful physical unit.

The problem that scientific certainty is a myth still struggles to brush past the academic prejudice of most scientists who are green on critical analysis for its alleged pedagogical irrelevance.

The challenge of measuring and quantifying immeasurable phenomena creates skepticism about the scientific nature of psychology as much as the scientific nature of all sciences, though.

Trial and error of *a priori* [rather than a posteriori] scientific theories is insufficient across the board, because of that the philosophers of science play up the blurred line between conceptual practice, and practice, science has blindly bargained on.

As we touched on at the beginning of the chapter, Thomas Kuhn lambasted Popper's analysis by inserting the concept of *paradigm shift* in his *The Structure of Scientific Revolutions,* released in 1962. In his opinion, a scientific community is not constituted on the back of a falsificationist methodology, but springs out of the uncritical and dogmatic acceptance of a way of thinking - a paradigm.

Kuhn divided the scientific process into two phases: normal science and extraordinary (or revolutionary) science. During the first phase, the majority of scientists work on the basis of [what they call] the current paradigm accepted by the scientific community, hunting Popper's ideas on falsifiability.

At this glade, says Kuhn, anomalies are created within the commonly accepted paradigm and phenomena, that models accepted by the scientific community are unable to spell out.

This parabola-shaped lava flow illustrates the application of mathematics in physics—in this case, Galileo's law of falling bodies. When enough anomalies accumulate, some scientists begin to work within the so-called "extraordinary science".

In this cycle, the impossibility of using the old models to explain reality is evident and new ones are sought (although most of them are destined to be refuted). Eventually, however, a new paradigm is created, and the old one is eliminated.

By thoroughly analyzing the passage between the old paradigm and the new one, Kuhn described his idea of demarcation: the new paradigm is commonly accepted, for it is able to better solve current problems (elitist authoritarianism).

Ultimately, the American historian and philosopher paved the way for the analysis of the subjectivity of scientific progress. This completely capsized when contemporary Paul Feyerabend published his most famous work, *Against the Method* (1975):

> "The fundamental characteristic of science is its rejection of any dogmatism, which translates into the openness to any methodology; any attempt to find an order in the world of science, by creating schemes to rigorously define the processes of research and discovery, is only doomed to failure, and this due to the intrinsic nature of the

path of discovery, which cannot be restricted or limited by the norms of a rigid method (problem of incommensurability)."

Barefaced, it seems that the supremacy of science as an objective, system of evaluation is unfounded, and it would, therefore, be appropriate to consider it as much as any ideology or superstition, limiting its pervasiveness and influence (epistemological anarchism).

The most belittled side to the scientific method is, in the concrete, creativity. Science makes progress when the physicist begins to imagine possibilities, the biologist welcomes armchair doubts, when scientists embrace divergent thinking (invention), that intellectual curiosity of a human race who does not know what the world holds, but takes up problem solving mysteries to remove the veil anyway (discoveries) and evolve, with the conviction that "the best way to predict the future is to create it" (Alan Kay).

Although mathematics is said to be the indisputable key tool and language, science is never the realm of certainty. The experimental method is simply a creative method that gained consensus, a scientific method *de riguer*.

Science is always the fruit of an ideal project, human's innate quality of imagination and the creative capacity of scientists, being curious people with higher mental power, thus it only apparently follows formality to achieve results, over time.

"I have no special talent. I am only passionately curious."

ALBERT EINSTEIN

Famous inventors like Thomas Alva Edison, Nikola Tesla, Guglielmo Marconi were subjected to subsequent, professional insulation by academic snobs.

Nowadays, a discovery takes place in the scientific field (pure research, carried out by researchers and scientists), while the invention more often occurs in the industrial fields, where the vision is an integral part of the technique.

Creativity constitutes the uniqueness of human beings compared to all other forms of life: we have improved civilization over the centuries, mostly by thinking and creating, rather than by experimenting or calculating, as naives are led to believe.

Technology does not always follow science but it may actually lead science, in some instances. A chief example is weather forecasting, a scientific research that is very dependent on technology, in the form of supercomputers.

Throughout the history, people were naturally inclined to the creative application of science and its methods, due to our notable inventiveness and originality, particularly triggered by practical and technical needs.

Stone tools was the earliest technology developed by humans for practicality. Engineering has existed since ancient times, when human beings devised fundamental inventions such as the pulley, lever, and wheel (ingenium means machine).

The Antikythera mechanism, the first known mechanical computer, and the mechanical inventions of Archimedes are exemplars of early mechanical engineering.

The pyramids in Egypt, the Acropolis and the Parthenon in Greece, Via Appia and the Colosseum, Teotihuacán, the Great Wall of China, the Brihadeeswarar Temple of Thanjavur, among many others, stand as a testament to the ingenuity and creative unawareness of ancient civil, and military engineers.

In 1901, Henry van de Velde flagged how the extraordinary beauty inherent in the work of engineers is developed on the absence of any awareness of its artistic possibilities – just as the creators of the cathedrals ignored the splendor of their creations.

In fact, human eclecticism confused, even if not directly, the historical figure of the architect and engineer, with respect to the role they have in civilization, sparking a disciplinary crisis whose effects have not yet been completely absorbed today.

Since Piranesi's dispute with the French Manette and LeRoy on the preeminence of the Romans over the Greeks, critics have long questioned whether the developers of the *urbs* - the Latin city par excellence, understood as the set of buildings and infrastructures - were architects or engineers, artists or technicians.

Classical world looked on "universal knowledge" as necessary for construction management, where branches of manufacturing and art marry.

In adding the dome to the Florence Cathedral (Italy) in the early 15th century, the architect Filippo Brunelleschi not only transformed the building and the city, but also the role and status of the architect.

The works of the Gothic craftsman, not only an engineer or technician but also the author of the design of mouldings, decoration, and of sculptural and pictorial works too, were the harbingers of the creativity-driven engineering process and heralded the prestige that engineers enjoy , in society, since the Ecole Polytechnique, inasmuch as formal novelty they are an unconscious expression of.

For the bulk of history, architecture is misconceived as subordinate to engineering, toward which it could only assume a decorative function, like humanities to sciences.

Despite the ambiguity of engineers who dismissed the innate quality of humans to construct "deliberately artistic buildings" or the contempt they accrued for hiding behind mathematics, the prejudice of the architects as squanderers of public money and reportedly being corrupted by tradition, long tarnished their recognition.

Their works were merely "wrong engineering": it suffices to add "just enough art" to give a look to the buildings.

Le Corbusier belaboured, in 1920, that engineers provide for the need and "make architecture" because they employ calculation derived from the laws of nature, so their works make us feel harmony.

The Renaissance intensified the idea of human genius and the work of art as the creation of autonomous personality: art is superior to tradition, to school, to the rule, to engineering itself, which actually draws from it its own law.

Leonardo da Vinci is a well-known Renaissance artist and engineer, a prime example of the nexus between art and engineering.

Nevertheless, the definitive split of the profession by 19th century drove a wedge between the engineers, those mainly oriented towards structural, technical aspects and the architects, those who focus more on aesthetics. The latter ended up to constitute, at best, an outgrowth of art.

> "A bicycle shed is a building. Lincoln Cathedral is a work of architecture."
>
> NIKOLAUS PEVSNER, 1943

An engineer, notwithstanding boasted the same unshakable faith in the power of reason that animated the architect Viollet-le-Duc, so much so that the Académie des Beaux-Arts, the artistic faculty of the Institut de France, in 1877, had to make yet another theoretical compromise, launching a competition on the merging of engineers and architects.

Winner of the Second Grand Prix, the architect Davioud famously intimated that the fusion would never become real, complete and fruitful, until the engineer - the artist and the scientist - was identified in the same person.

Construction, in general, can be defined as the development of buildings for practical purposes but this does not mean, however, that a building be bereft of "beauty" connotations.

Unforgettable are the fights the engineer Gustav Eiffel waged for his plan to build the eponymous, iron tower - now symbol of Paris and the global icon of France - against the glorious architect Jules Bourdais's competing project in expensive granite.

The Akashi Kaikyō Bridge in Japan, currently the world's longest suspension span.

The objections against Eiffel Tower were yet another testimony of the long-standing competition between architecture and engineering, and the most tangible academic spin-off, in the history, of the low social respect humanities suffer when pitted against science.

Winning was the engineer who, whilst lacking the artistic skills of the architects, bet on solid technical, economic and construction preparation including borrowing on industrial materials, unbeknownst to the fine art of architecture.

<<The architecture of engineers>>, as it was promptly baptised, was the highest, involuntary expression of a "democratization of architecture" within engineering or more precisely the onset of "structural art".

Gropius, in 1923, lambasted the architects for overestimating their own "utility", while the engineer, unhindered by aesthetic or historical prejudices, achieved clear, organic forms, in recorded history.

The architects of rationalism consequently strove to remove any artistic velleity from the concept of architecture, in favour of works engaged for utility, and service to the public.

Architecture rebounded as *beauty, stability and utility*, pushing those labile boundaries that the rivalry with engineering has imposed, to remark how beauty inspires engineering and that architecture is not just art, but the art of building.

Civil engineering and architecture decoupling is the paternalistic university writ large and the divide would keep the pulse on the subject until 1930, when disciplinary and professional disagreements faded in the magma of institutional silence and academic specialization.

An influential critique of the concept of academic disciplines came from Michel Foucault in his 1975 book, *Discipline and Punish*. Foucault asserted that academic disciplines grow out of the same social movements and mechanisms of control, that established the modern prison and penal system in 18-century France; his thesis reveals essential aspects they continue to have in common.

> "The disciplines characterize, classify, specialize; they distribute along a scale, around a norm, hierarchize individuals in relation to one another and, if necessary, disqualify and invalidate."
>
> FOUCAULT, 1975/1979, P. 223

Lakatos, more than anyone, re-evaluated the role of metaphysics in science, noting how scientific theories are made up of fundamental parts that can never be tested, nor be falsifiable. Metaphysics, consequently, is science and cannot be excluded from the scientific debate, since scientific progress is only a creative process, driven by the considerable ingenuity of humankind, whose hypotheses are accepted as accurate, when they explain better the reality.

Enfin, when scientific research strives to achieve final "metaphysical" objectives, it always uses them as stimula to push the achievement of more and more in-depth knowledge, ever further.

The demarcation is now reduced to the analysis of the continuity of scientific theories, that is, to the distinction between those research methods that Lakatos defined as *"regressive programs"* and those methods that spawn progress, labeled as *"progressive programs"*.

> **DID YOU KNOW?** ▼

> Aristotle, the father of **biology**, described five major biological processes from collected observations: metabolism, temperature regulation, inheritance, information processing and embryogenesis. His successor, Theophrastus, began the scientific study of plants (**botanics**) and its parts (development of **anatomy** and **embryology**).

> Water can boil & freeze at the same time and a cockroach has the ability to live for up to one week without its head.

> When we touch something, we send a message to our brain at 124 mph. Nerve impulses travel at over 400 km/hr (249 mi/hr). Our heart beats around 100,00 times every day or about 30 million times a year. Our blood is on a 60,000-mile journey per day. We exercise at least 36 muscles when we smile. There is more bacteria in your mouth than the human population of the United States or Canada.

# CHAPTER IX

# Language

*Meaning and Reference*

---

How does language refer to the real world and truth?

---

Language refers to reality by expressing facts and opinions. Through the principal method of human communication, people are able to form a shared interpretation of their experience with the world around them. Without language, it would be impossible to hand over information accurately, as language allows for an abstract representation of concepts and ideas, conveyed by speech, writing, or gesture to be understood by many.

By telling about the real world and real life, language serves to create knowledge and truth, enabling individuals to make sense of how the world works, and how they should act and react to it.

Language is capable of generating and transferring information, by establishing an interactive relationship of symbols with identical value for individuals belonging to the same socio-cultural environment. World languages are, as we know, an important part of personal and collective identity, reflecting origins, values and beliefs.

All animal species use various channels to communicate: the house mouse (*Mus musculus*), for example, employs olfactory signals to communicate to another mouse its own sex, or the family group they belong to; they adopt visual signals (posing the body in a particular way, and vibrating or not the tail) when they want to convey aggressive or submissive intentions; and in youth, they rhythmically emit ultrasounds to be found by the mother.

The number of signals used by a species (vocabulary) and the complexity of the language that stems from them are in direct proportion to the degree of social organization. Complex and perfected languages are found in social insects (termites, ants, bees) but even animals belonging to species with simpler social relationships appear to have a fairly varied vocabulary: the chaffinch (*Fringilla coelebs*), for instance, has 14 basic songs, which may vary producing 21 different signals.

The primary difference between human and animal languages is that human language is symbolic, whereas animal communication does not involve symbols.

Much communication between non-human species has reproductive purposes or conquest and defense of an area (territoriality) for such. A frequent rule is that, for the recognition and synchronization of the sexes, the male initiates the emission of specific signals (courtship); these signals often concern the shape or colour of the animal (*Phasianids*, birds-of-paradise, certain Coleoptera).

In the fireflies (*Lampyridae*), the single species emit luminous flashes which are distinguished, by the rhythm, intensity and by the colour. In turtles (*Testudines*) recognition occurs through tactile signals: the males tap the carapace of the females with a different rhythm for each species. Acoustic signals are frequent (*Anuran amphibians*, nocturnal birds, insects) as well as chemical ones (many species of mammals and insects).

Numerous insects produce specific chemicals to attract individuals of the opposite sex from great distances. It suffices that a few molecules of the substance emitted come into contact with the receptors of an individual of the opposite sex, for one to go in the right direction. For the male red cockroach (*Periplaneta americana*) and for the silk moth (*Bombyx mori*), contact with 10–4μg, about 30 molecules, is enough.

A type of animal communication that is generally transmitted from parents to offspring concerns the approach of a predator.

Communicating the presence of accumulations of food substances is another widely used mechanism of social cooperation: gibbons, vultures, gulls, partridges, flies, ants and bees, to name but a few. In the latter species (*Apis mellifica*) we witness the maximum complexity and perfection.

Often, the transmission of information takes place between individuals of different species, such as the fish *Labroides dimidiatus*, feeding on the ectoparasites they remove from the fins of other fish *Plectorhyncus diagrammus*. In response to particular optical signals, the latter assume an inviting position, while the former respond with a dance.

Through exchange of "passwords", the fish recognize this and let themselves be freed from the parasites. Another fish (*Aspidontus taeniatus*), similar to *Labroides*, simulates the signals of *Labroides* to be accepted in its place, but instead of freeing the fishes from the parasites, they devour its fins.

In certain birds (Fringilla, Vanellus) different alarm signals exist depending on whether the predator creeps up on from the sky or from the ground, carrying different defense reactions. Some grasshoppers emit a small sound (signal of departure) when they take a leap.

Human language is much more complex and sophisticated than animal communication: it is generative, because humans can use language to create and express new ideas, while animal communication is primarily limited to these instinctive and habitual responses. While animal communication is used primarily to communicate practical needs, human language can convey abstract concepts.

Natural language is a system of symbolic communication used by people to express thoughts, feelings, and ideas (systematic communication).

Among the animal codes and the many non-verbal or artificial codes shaped by human species, the class of historical-natural languages stands out for its peculiarities.

Vocality is not a necessary feature of the verbal language. The fact that linguistic signs can and are, in the concrete, realized graphically, sometimes also mimicly and often endophonically, proves that vocality is not a prerequisite for language.

The phonic-acoustic realization of a message does not hinder (unlike graphic or mimic realizations) the execution of other human activities; these are possible in any lighting condition and can be modulated in terms of frequency, with respect to signals of an optical-luminous type. All this helps to explain why the human species has cleverly adopted in its evolution signals of a phonic-acoustic type to realize the signifier of linguistic signs.

Cuneiform is the first known form of written language, but spoken language predates writing by at least many tens of thousands of years.

Spoken language is, among the various forms, the one that allows the greatest complexity and speed of information transmission.

The information human beings learned to transmit have three functions:

- to express the state and intentions of the speaker (expression)
- to influence who receives them (recall)
- to inform about things (representation)

Philosophical reflection on language hails from the archaic belief in the powers of the divine and human word: in the Vedic hymn to Vac (*"the Voice"*), all things in the universe appear pervaded by an intrinsic vocality and resound with their name; in the beginning of Genesis, the biblical divinity does not create by doing, but simply by speaking.

Widespread was the belief and magical practice whereby knowledge of the name of a person or thing confers dominion over it; hence, for example, among the Aztecs the habit of a double imposition of the name, one secret and one public.

Aristotle underscored language as the basis for reason and, in its partitions and structures, being human reflection of partitions and structures of reality, therefore language is privileged access to knowledge.

With this notion, language began to acquire a conventional and unnatural character in framing human experience. The emergence of vernaculars in the Middle Ages, in fact, generated awareness of the specific, historically peculiar link between each idiom and each people and historical age.

In the language of a species, modifications considered dialects may appear. This has been spotted in butterflies (chemical language), in birds (acoustic language) and in bees. In the latter, case in point, a difference was found between German and Italian female explorers in the way of signalling the distance of the forage from the hive. Studies have smoked out that when an Italian explorer is accepted into a German beehive, they give information that is misinterpreted by the German working bees, who thus go to the wrong point.

In the *Convivio* and in *De vulgari eloquentia,* Dante Alighieri supplied the first documents on the historicization of languages, bound to become more precise with the European thought of the 17th and 18th centuries.

For scientific classification, the discriminating moment for a linguistic system to be considered dialect it is not only its opposition to a national language or culture, but also its belonging to a genetically compact group of systems, determined through a complex of substantially common innovations, and additions.

Anatomo-clinical research on human language was stimulated by the French surgeon Paul Broca, who obtained evidence of the presence of an articulated language center in an area of the left cerebral hemisphere of two subjects who had lost the ability to express themselves verbally, whilst retaining the ability to understand what was being said and to reply with gestures.

Soviet psychologists and neurolinguists such as A.R. Luria, A.N. Sokolov, L.S. Vygotsky later determined the existence of an inner language - a soundless language - which constitutes the form of human thought in mental words. The electromyograph has made it possible to highlight an increase in the tone of the vocal muscles during inner speech and to carry out important investigations on the thinking of the deaf, on auditory hallucinations ("voices") as well as on toneless reading.

Pathology increasingly availed language, particularly its incoherence, as expressive indication of serious disorders of the ideational course, like schizophrenia.

Against the trend of reducing language to a neurophysiological phenomenon subdivided into elementary components (motor, auditory and visual), neurologist John H. Jackson carefully analyzed the process of verbalization and contributed greatly, with Henry Head, to the idea of language as a trans and subcortical, functionally integrated system.

> On this basis, there are a series of distinctive features of human language, namely:
>
> 1. **Productivity:** Humans can produce and understand an infinite number of utterances, even though the number of words in their vocabulary is finite.
> 2. **Displacement:** Human language can talk about events that occurred in the past or may occur in the future, or that are happening at a different location from where the speaker is currently located.
> 3. **Arbitrariness:** There is no logical reason why a particular word means what it does.
> 4. **Double articulation:** We use two levels of sound segments to create meaning. The first is morphemes (the smallest unit of meaning), and the second is phonemes (the smallest unit of sound).
> 5. **Prevarication:** We often use language to tell lies or exaggerate the truth, in order to get our own way.
> 6. **Metalinguistic awareness:** We are able to reflect on the

> properties and use of language, as demonstrated by children's use of "meta-discourse" such as "I said...".

The study of language, called *linguistics*, has a long tradition, with antiquity as its inception. In the late 19th century, scholars launched into a systematic study of language, blended by traditional philological studies and examination of structural, and functional aspects of language. This handbrake turn was pioneered by scholars such as Franz Boas and Edward Sapir in North America, and Ferdinand de Saussure and Leonard Bloomfield in Europe.

In the early 20th century, Noam Chomsky and Ronald Langacker, among others, inaugurated theories of generative grammar that sought to explain the underlying structure of language. More recently, linguists have focused on describing and analyzing the various aspects of language structure and usage, both in order to understand its structure and to construct computer systems that are able to process natural language. Turing machines, first described by Alan Turing in Turing 1936–7, are simple abstract computational devices intended to help investigate the extent and limitations of what can be thought.

Basic constituent structure analysis of a sentence:

```
              Sentence
             /        \
                    Predicate / Verb Phrase
                    /         \
                            Prepositional Phrase
                            /        \
        Noun Phrase                  Noun Phrase
        /     \      |       |       /      \
   Article  Noun   Verb  Preposition Article  Noun
     |      |      |       |         |       |
    The    cat    sat      on       the     mat.
```

*In addition to word classes, a sentence can be analyzed in terms of grammatical functions: "The cat" is the subject of the phrase, "on the mat" is a locative phrase, and "sat" is the core of the predicate.*

The English mathematician went on to unconsciously make fundamental contributions to computer science, theoretical biology and cryptography. These efforts have been aided by advances in technology, such as the development of artificial intelligence and natural language processing.

For the last sixty years and more, computational methods and language models have been growing in importance for linguistics, and algorithms for processing human language have attained progressively greater abilities, and disabilities.

Computers process our commands using programming language, for instance translations but we increasingly need machines to understand our own natural language too, that is, not just words but the meaning behind them, the context, the patterns such as humour.

Human linguistic performance or any human linguistic act, in sooth, floats on the distinction between what is said explicitly and what is implicitly assumed. This is also why we argue with each other or misunderstand for persuasion or power dynamics, by the way.

The words and structures of the implicit part of human language normally convey something more or different than what the expression means. So if there is an implicit part of human language, how can we produce something that makes sense? The answer is still up in the air.

Within the purview of this, the Turing test, the ultimate test for a machine to be called intelligent, is also a language test for human beings.

The analysis and description of the multiple possible interrelationships between individual perceptive and cognitive phenomena set the scene for the research of the poetic, journalistic, literary, ritual and legal use of languages in historical settings.

---

The main theories of philosophy of language resulted to be:

**1. Semantic Theories:** These theories focus on the meaning of words, and how words come to have the meanings that they do. This type of theory is mainly based on the work of philosophers such as Frege and Russell.

**2. Pragmatic Theories:** These theories focus on how language is used in communication, including the role context and intention in conveying meaning. This type of theory is often based on the work of philosophers such as Austin and Grice.

**3. Cognitive Theories:** These theories focus on how language is processed by our cognitive systems, including the role of unconscious information and context in understanding. This type of theory is often developed on the work of researchers such as Chomsky, Fodor, and Harnish.

**4. Discourse Theories:** These theories focus on how language is used in different contexts, and how this use changes the way we interact with each other and think about the world. This type of theory is often evolved from the work of scholars such as Habermas, Foucault and Derrida.

Philosophical theories of reference attempt to explain how words acquire specific meanings: an account of how people come to refer to particular entities within their environment. There are two main kinds of theories: the direct reference theory and the description theory.

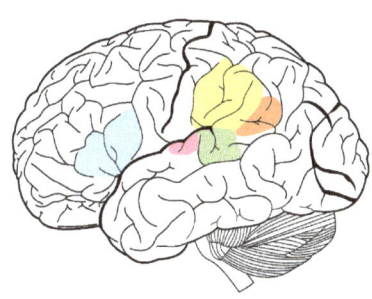

**Language Areas of the brain.**
*The Angular Gyrus is represented in orange, Supramarginal Gyrus is represented in yellow, Broca's area is represented in blue, Wernicke's area is represented in green, and the Primary Auditory Cortex is represented in pink.*

According to the direct reference theory, words refer directly to objects or concepts in the world. This theory states that words are associated to certain entities through a kind of "mental ostension", whereby the speaker is acutely aware of what they are referring to. This theory was developed by Gottlob Frege and Bertrand Russell in the early 20th century as the core of the analytic philosophy's linguistic turn and development of modern logic.

The description theory of reference was first proposed by Gottlob Frege. Proponents hold that the meaning of words is not found in any particular objects or concepts, but rather in the series of descriptions wed with them.

This suggests that we learn to use words based on their semantic content (sense) and contextual understanding (reference). This theory has been nursed by philosophers such as Saul Kripke, who argued that some terms (what he called "rigid designators") refer to the same set of things, no matter what the context.

There is arbitrariness in communication, any way we shape the topic: both the form of the meaning and that of the signifier of the signs (such as a sound, printed word or image) do not count on any reason of a natural type, rather only on the relationship that the speakers establish between the different meanings, and the different signifiers of the language (F. de Saussure calls it *radical arbitrariness*).

Equally unmotivated, and therefore cannot be traced back to any type of convention, is consequently the "reference" between meaning, that should not be confused with the concept, and the signifier, which should not be confused with the whole word.

# *Meaning and Communication*

---

Do people think in language or do they think and then learn to translate those thoughts
into language, tolerating indeterminacy?

---

Meaning and reference are related terms within the field of linguistics. Meaning is the concept that is transmitted by a word, phrase, sentence or text, whereas reference is the way words are used to stand for real-world objects, events and people. Put it simply, meaning is what the words mean and reference is how we use those words to refer to real-world things.

The problem of meaning is the struggle to define and accurately interpret the meaning of words and language. Meaning is often subjective and can be interpreted differently by different people, in different situations. This controversy makes it thorny for individuals to communicate effectively, which can lead to daily misunderstandings and conflicts.

Natural language is a fundamental notion in philosophy of language. It pertains to the everyday language adopted by individuals in their day-to-day lives to communicate with others. Ordinary language is typically recognised as the primary medium for carrying meaning and expressing ideas - the primary means of understanding and interpreting the world around us by a process of use, repetition and change, without conscious planning or premeditation.

One of the key wrangles in philosophy of language focuses on whether natural language has an objective meaning or meaning is determined by individual perspectives and experiences. Those who believe in objective meaning argue that natural language has precise and fixed definitions that can be objectively determined. In contrast, those who believe in subjective meaning argue that sense is inherently subjective and influenced by individual perspectives and experiences.

A conversation in American Sign Language

Semantics is concerned with the study of the meaning of words and how they are used in language. Philosophers who study semantics strive to figure out the relationships between words, concepts and the world around us.

The parallel between language and thought is impugned. Some claim that language precedes thought because it gives a structure for ideas organization and expression. Others insist that thought predates because we create and manipulate mental representations, before putting them into words. Ultimately, there is no clear consensus on which one comes first.

It is likely that people think in language as well as other concepts, images and emotions. Language appears to be a primary form of thought for many individuals, because it allows for more structured and cohesive ideas than non-linguistic forms of communication. However, for some people, non-linguistic forms are more readily accessible and/or easier to express.

In that event, there may be indeterminacy in the translation of thoughts into language, due to a variety of factors such as cultural context, personal experiences and individual speech patterns.

Social interaction is to language what the window is to a room and for this reason, communication gets complicated.

Relay almost always imply the participation of two or more subjects, completely different to each other train of thought (or interpretation), otherwise a soliloquy takes place - the Latin root *communicare* purposely means *"to share"*.

One may think reasoning (or rational discourse) suffices to deal with misunderstanding in a shared context but the link between logic and language is fundamentally complex, and unhelpful.

At embryonic level, logic is the study of reasoning and argumentation, whereas language indicates the system of signs and symbols used for communication. How-

Arnold Lakhovsky, The Conversation (c. 1935)

ever, the two are intimately intertwined in philosophical inquiry, since language is the primary expedient we express and articulate our logical and conceptual insights by.

A chief philosophical tradition that explores this bond is formal logic, which endeavours to develop a precise and rigorous system of rules for reasoning and inference. In this bodywork, language functions as a kind of syntax or grammar for logical analysis, in order for human beings to construct valid arguments and reason about abstract concepts with clarity, and accuracy.

Feedback on the connection between logic and language accrued in the field of linguistic philosophy, with an emphasis on the role of language in shaping our interpretation of the humankind. In this setting, language is not simply a tool for expressing intentions and concepts, rather the channel we make sense of and decode reality itself.

The association between logic and language in philosophy is still an odyssey, favouring a multiplex intersection between the fields of language, logic, cognition and culture.

By the same token, translation and interpretation can be challenging because of the polarity between languages, cultures and nuances. It is not just about finding equivalent words or phrases, but also about gathering the context, tone and intention of the message.

**The Tower of Babel by Pieter Bruegel the Elder. Oil on board, 1563.**
*Humans have speculated about the origins of language throughout history. The Biblical myth of the Tower of Babel is one such account; other cultures have different stories of how language arose*

Cultural differences can make it onerous to pass on certain concepts accurately, and idiomatic expressions may not have direct translations. Contrast to grammar, syntax, and pronunciation can affect the meaning of a sentence, to boot.

These tests require translators and interpreters to have a deep notion of both the source and target language, as well as the cultural contexts in which they are used. Machine translation and interpretation tools are seldom reliable, and may produce errors or inaccuracies that could have a significant impact on communication into the bargain.

Vagueness is a landmark philosophical concept that addresses the lack of precision or clarity in human language, postulations or ideas across logic, epistemology and metaphysics.

In the realm of language, vagueness is often expressed through the use of ambiguous or imprecise terms like "some", "many" or "almost." These labels can have multiple connotations, aggravating the miscomprehension of their precise meaning.

In epistemology, vagueness describes the brain-twister of how much certainty we can have about our knowledge of the world. To illustrate, there may be cases where it is unclear whether a certain object belongs to a particular category or not, leading to uncertainty about the truth of our beliefs.

In metaphysics, ambiguity shows up in discussions about the nature of reality and its boundaries. To give you an idea, the concept of time is frequently vague because it is arduous to pin down exactly what it is, and where it begins and ends.

Vagueness is time and again juggled between philosophers as a problem, on account of confusion and disharmony over the proper inference of beliefs and propositions. Be that as it may, vagueness reflects a constitutional aspect of human thought and language, and cannot be completely eliminated.

In line with this, a major philosophical perspective emphasized the importance of subjective experience and consciousness in communication, and social interaction.

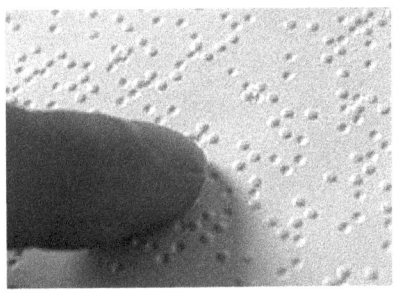

**Braille**
*a tactile writing system*

The theory observes that people perceive the world through their lived experiences, which shape their understanding and analysis of social interactions (phenomenology).

Existentialism, its precursor fringe, stressed human freedom and the responsibility to make one's own choices in communication and social interaction, intensifying that individuals must take responsibility for their actions and be aware of their impact on others.

Chomsky brought to the fore that all human beings are born with an innate knowledge of language, which he referred to as *Universal Grammar*. For the renowned linguist, this innate ability to learn and use language is hard-wired into our brains and is responsible for our ability to acquire language quickly, and effectively.

His theory of generative grammar also foregrounded that language is not just a set of learned responses to stimuli but is instead generated by a set of rules that govern its structure and use. These rules are part of the innate capacity for language that all human beings possess.

Chomsky dwelled on a special module present in the human brain called the Language Acquisition Device, which enables us to learn and use language. This device is programmed with the rules of Universal Grammar and helps us to generate, and understand grammatically correct sentences.

Social constructionism encouraged, on the other hand, that language and social interaction are socially constructed, that is, they are shaped by the cultural, historical and anthropological contexts within they occur.

Broadview, this philosophy argues that all reality is created and sustained through communication, and social interaction.

**Wall of Love on Montmartre in Paris**
*"I love you" in 250 languages, by calligraphist Fédéric Baron and artist Claire Kito (2000)*

A disrupting spinout of social constructionism rallies against social structures and power relations as the core of the problematic status quo between language and society.

Critical theory, in fact, advocates the role of power and oppression shapes these constant interactions, hence gauging language and social interaction in a critical way reveal and challenge inequalities, toxic habits, unconscious bias, injustices.

Nonetheless, people still prefer to address the most practical consequences of language and society, rather than diving too deep and hammer away at a plot.

In this style, pragmatism convinced that we should focus on what works best, in specific situations and adapt our communication strategies accordingly, to achieve our practical goals.

## DID YOU KNOW? ▼

*"I Am"* is the shortest complete sentence in the English language.

**'Pneumonoultramicroscopicsilicovolcanoconiosis'** is one of the world's longest words and the shortest grammatically correct sentence is the command "Go!", where the subject isn't written or spoken, yet it is immediately understood.

If you repeat a word or phrase repeatedly up to about 30 times, it will lose its meaning to the listener. Then it will sound like a meaningless word or sound (**semantic satiation**).

# CHAPTER X

# Aesthetics

## Taste and Theory of Beauty

---

Is beauty universal?
Can aesthetic judgments be "subjectively universal"?

---

Beautiful is an adjective we repeatedly abuse to indicate something we like. Aesthetics is the discipline that studies the nature of beauty and its perception by people (from the Greek *aisthētikós*), which is why it is closely linked to Art.

Since childhood, we are taught that beauty is the scepter of a woman or a man and the mind must therefore be modeled on the body, evanesce in this golden cage.

First reflections date back to Xenophon of Athens who defined beauty as collectively ideal, functional and spiritual, depending on the external point of view.

Plato articulated beauty as harmony and order, influenced by the Pythagorean rationalism. However, for the philosopher, beauty had an autonomous existence and did not correspond to what is seen (idealist world-view). As a result, Beauty coincided with the very idea of Good (*kalakogathia*) and Truth.

Art is nothing more than an imitation of nature (mimesis), which in turn is an imitation of the idea, therefore an imitation of imitation - not a direct expression of beauty.

Taking issue with the transcendence of Platonic ideas, Aristotle evolved a theory of beauty that is a broader theory of art, including natural objects too and not just artistic products. In his view, *abyssus abyssum invocat*, an object is beautiful when it fully achieves its purpose (or form).

While the artworks create their purpose, that is intrinsic in the natural entities: the human form (and therefore beauty) is the adult condition or achievement of the universal.

**The bust of Nefertiti, 14th century BC**

Agreed that, beauty continued to reflect order and measure such as arrangement or organicity, so it did not simply refer to external features, rather to its suitability to the form.

In the imitative and mimetic nature of art, Aristotle therefore saw no reason to consider it illusory, as Plato did.

The world imitated by the artist, arguendo, is no longer a simple appearance but a reality that can be the object of knowledge through the mediated understanding of the intellect, which illuminates its purpose. The artist's task is not to represent things as they really are but as they could be.

Any aesthetic experience is an exercise in taste, the ability to grasp and appreciate beauty.

Its concept from the genesis is philosophically correlated with pleasure, that is, to subjectivity, made up of inclinations and passions, autonomous with respect to pure rationality.

The concepts of beauty based on the Greco-Roman principle of symmetry and harmony spread in the Middle Ages, especially thanks to the work of Boethius.

From the 18th century, the attitude of individual judgment that acquires the shared character of universality would seem to be inherent in the concept of taste.

For Voltaire, as for Montesquieu, there is both the intuitive faculty of grasping beauty and the reason that comes to define it analytically in taste. Turning point of these philosophical reflections came with Kant's *Critique of Judgment*.

Kant proclaimed that what is universally liked without concept is beautiful. Beauty is "the object of a pure aesthetic judgment", that is the object of an aesthetic pleasure, independent of any form of interest and disconnected from any conceptuality.

Taste is, ab ovo, based on the possibility of universal agreement with other subjects (*"universally communicable"*) and is not collateral to the object itself but to that aesthetic activity, which is an autonomous sphere of our way of feeling.

Ergo, aesthetic judgments are "subjectively universal".

The judgment of taste is "not a judgment of knowledge; it is therefore not logical, but aesthetic". It follows that "the principle of determination can only be subjective" (*Critique of Judgment*, in *Analytic of Aesthetic judgment*).

For Kant, beauty represented a very particular predicate: it does not determine anything about the object of which it is predicated, inversely expresses something about the subject alone who formulates the judgment in question.

In nuce, beauty is the predicate of a judgment: an aesthetic judgment whereby nothing is known about the represented object, rather the expression of the relationship between the perceiving subject and his feeling of pleasure.

Amplifying the Aristotelian abstraction on beauty, Kant essentially claimed that the subject only spotlights a *representation* of the beautiful.

If I stand in front of a red rose and make the judgment "the rose is red", I underscore a quality of the object (synthetic judgments) but if you claim "this rose is beautiful", you formalize, instead, the aesthetic pleasure of the experience.

Such is, first and foremost, a pure or "disinterested" experience, for the judgment of taste shall not be contaminated by an inclination, or rather by an interest in the object.

Pleasure is enjoyment interested in the existence of the object and its possession (subjectivism), while beauty is disinterested contemplation (what pleases, without concept), whilst being radically subjective - a universal voice of a universally shareable pleasure (subjective universality).

Beauty, as defined by George Santayana, is an "objectified pleasure" (*The Sense of Beauty*, 1896).

Yet searching for a possible universal rule on what is beautiful and ugly still appears desperate and often inconclusive.

Noting the great variety of tastes, David Hume exemplified that the rules of taste, like all the others, are *a posteriori* (discoverable from experience), since an object is beautiful, only based on the sentiment that binds it to the subject in the aesthetic experience - which relates their universality with the subjectivity Kant took in.

The meaning of Art and Beauty matured in the history of taste, without coinciding, yet with reciprocal influences.

Across the ages, the concept of Beauty has always been temporal and subjective. Beautiful were the monstrosities of the Middle Ages to a mistic or the harmony of the celestial spheres in the Renaissance. Beauty took on anomalous forms in Romanticism, to the point of believing that a love that is stretched until pain is beautiful, thus creating the literary *topos* love-death, because beauty was everything that shocks the senses and the soul (Sturm und Drang).

Beautiful has also become an artifice and diversion in the decadent twentieth century or even a joking topic, desecration for the Crepusculars.

To a craftsman, his vase is beautiful and so is a barbershop to the barber, a son to his mother but these instances do not rise to the dignity of beauty, as we intend it in society, until art represents them. Even a reproduction of the ugly or of nature in a storm can be beautiful.

Art is often the prerogative of a few that still determines "the universality of a beauty" such as when a painter gives prominence to a selected woman in a portrait which enhances her own beauty or an actor constantly being in the media spotlight makes his unique beauty gradually "everyone's taste".

A significant point to remember, in fact, is that the Beautiful in Nature is an unconscious event (natural or relative beauty), while the Beautiful in Art is the conscious work of a personality (aesthetic or universal beauty).

Ugliness is a spurious antonym and something is deemed ugly only for universal disagreements, not for particular faults (social stigma of difference). It follows that beauty is surely perceived by those who are not artists too but in order to be pure as a concept, it must not only be conceived in art (e.g. cosmetic) but also in nature (i.e. realistic).

Contrary to what many would think today, for an artist of the time, between a naked woman and a dressed one, the naked woman (Venus) embodied sacred love, as being natural, whereas the dressed woman (the bride) the profane.

If beauty is therefore truth, more than aesthetics, then intense pleasure comes to those who ditch the common pleasure apt for dormant, carnal mechanicity and set their mind to Plato's *scala amoris*, whereby a warm soul intensely rises from desire towards the disinterested contemplation of female beauty - true pleasure is giving without receiving.

What powers modern aesthetic reflection is the recognition that art and beauty are individual, and historical notions.

The goddess Venus (Aphrodite) is the classical personification of beauty.
The Birth of Venus (c. 1485) by Sandro Botticelli

A work is, traditionally, considered Art based on its purposeless Beauty - "art for art's sake" (aestheticism), subject to its ability to providing pleasure (hedonistic theories of art), for its epistemic role in achieving truth or knowledge or, more subtly, by virtue of its function in our moral development (moralism).

A complete definition of "moral art" does not exist and current laws establish the freedom of Art from any function.

For some, it is necessary to judge a work, without neglecting the intentionality of the artist during the creative act, with benchmark to our socio-historical system (moral criticism). However, such must emerge clearly, regardless of the recipient's subjective interpretation and irrelevant moral considerations (ethical autonomists).

The artist is able to protect the work from any disputes by bringing out his real artistic will. With *Pinxit*, aesthetic freedom can be safeguarded and adequately protected by interested practical attitudes, which sometimes risk compressing excessively the artist's expressive space.

# Human and Artistic Expressions

Do we experience genuine emotions toward works of art?
What is the role of "emotion" in aesthetics?

Epistemological problems of perception entail an aesthetic paradox, thus it became titanic to describe whether art is representation or just a form of expression.

Throughout the history, art is, at the same time, in search of beauty and the representation or transmission of "significant aspects of the human experience", alias, what concerns fundamental aspects of life, attributable to the great themes and problems of existence (Arnheim).

The most famous example may be Vincent Van Gogh's *"The Starry Night"*. The painter did not represent what he had really seen, but as his soul perceived those stars in the night sky - ergo, what he felt by looking at the sky.

Aesthetics, from the original meaning of the term *aisthesis* (sensation) was originally defined as "the artist's intuition-expression, whose work is a consideration of the real and an image of the possible" (Benedetto Croce, *Aesthetics as a Science of Expression and General Linguistics*, 1902).

For all to see, art is not a form to a content but an expression of the individual: intuition, knowledge of the particular and as such, an autonomous spiritual and theoretical activity.

The distinction between art and non-art nowadays lies in the degree of intensity of that intuition-expression. We all sense and express but the artist has a stronger, richer and deeper intuition to match an adequate expression.

At the core, art uses beauty, emotion and drama to influence the audience into expressing their feelings. R.G. Collingwood argued this is not an object that you can fabricate, rather art is the expression of emotion in your mind.

However, the English philosopher defended that the act of making art was more than just *naive expressivism:* art is a vehicle of emotions between author and appreciator.

With the musical phenomenon philosophically driving a formal analysis of its linguistic model ("sonic forms in motion"), music, more than other forms of art, appeared to "possess" expressive qualities (Kyvi, 1980), somewhat bearing a resemblance to a "language" of emotion.

Under these circumstances, Collingwood and many others, believed that when producing, the artist does not have yet the aesthetic emotion that the work will produce in the public; there is only an "emotional excitement", which is an incomprehensible feeling.

Philosophers like him suspected that the emotion felt by the spectator is an aesthetic emotion, far superior to the emotion that the artist feels when experiencing a certain act, which stimulates the production of a certain artistic composition.

In the fullness of time, thought and imagination resulted to be as important as the expression of feelings in artistic-making.

To use Sartre's words:

> "The imagination constitutes an unreal object, it is nothing but the negation of reality and the tension towards another world".

In the last thirty years, Roger Scruton humoured the French existentialist and noted how music is made up of tones, which we perceive [exemplify] as sound through imaginative metaphors - the bases of our emotional response - a notion further developed as "metaphorical exemplification" by Goodman's semiotic theory.

Idealist overtones advanced with Wollheim's theory of the correspondence, whose major tenet argued that the perception of expressive qualities of art (expressive perception) is the product of a complex projection by the spectators. Barefaced, a painting is, at best, pictorial representation. This, in short time, promoted the institutionalization of Art.

Imagination organizes the author's feelings and also serves the public, to interpret and understand the feelings contained in the work. Art is, therefore, capable of bringing "presentational symbols" forward to enable better interpretation of the world: what Langer refers to as *symbolic interaction*.

To give further impetus to the thesis, the paradox of fiction or emotional response towards works of art asked why we experience strong emotions when, for instance, we are watching a horror movie while, at the same time, we recognize that nothing is real and yet we are being "afraid of nothing".

> The solutions proposed here are interesting and mostly consist in denying:
>
> A. that something must exist for it to cause us an emotion, since its mental representation is sufficient (**theory of thought**);
> B. that we know that the artistic content (characters, situations, etc.) is actually real and we sacrifice realism and logic - the so-called "willing suspension of disbelief" - just to fully enjoy the fiction (**theory of illusion**);
> C. that our emotions during the experience are genuine, being far less intense than those we might feel in real

> life - *quasi-emotions*, Walton - therefore, we pretend these "second-order" beliefs are true (**simulation theory**).

Sticking to these principles, it is possible to "fake" a belief or an emotion, yet the fiction of an artwork also conveys moral values: drama, for one, engages us far beyond the emotions it arouses, flexing our ethical conscience.

Reflections of this kind beget further inquiries on why we enjoy, in fiction, what is naturally painful and terrible: why tragedy attracts us more than beauty and why such negative emotions, in the end, are pleasant.

The first solution is to assert that the pleasure resulting from any tragic show outweighs the suffering. The second states that the search for pain is an attempt to reach *catharsis*, which is a form of liberation from those negative emotions.

Aristotle formerly outlined the concept as a purification of the spectators, who experience pity, fear, disgust during the tragic drama, by identifying themselves with the pain through imitation. Shockingly, he concluded, when an artwork represents "ugliness", it produces pain yet has poetic value.

The painting depicts a group of monks laughing while a lone monk struggles with an ass.
*Return to the Convent, by Eduardo Zamacois y Zabala, 1868*

The closely related *Schadenfreude*, a borrowed word from German (*Schaden* is damage/harm and *Freude* means joy) refers to the experience of pleasure, joy or self-satisfaction that comes from learning of, or witnessing the troubles, failures, or humiliation of another. Social scientists Shamay-Tsoory, Ahronberg-Kirschenbaum and Bauminger-Zviely quite recently detected such apparent, neighbourhood-only phenomenon, in children as young as twenty-four months and discovered that it may be an important social emotion establishing "inequity aversion".

From day one, the paradoxical equation between ugliness and attraction has branded human beings, who socio-psychologically display propensity for fear, harm, cruelty - that greatness which has the power to destroy (the *Sublime* - Edmund Burke 1757), as opposed to a putative passion for love and what is aesthetically pleasing (Beauty) traditionally dispatching perfectionism.

Wittgenstein believed only language could give meaning to pain but Schopenhauer still resonates reflecting that:

> "Our will to live, continuously objectified by longing for what we lack, what is greater - the desire for the Sublime, our will to power - creates tension and goes in direct proportion to suffering".

In agreement with this and a rich literary consensus, contemporary philosophers like Berys Gaut infer that "being in awe or pain, in some circumstances can be a source of enjoyment". That is, the way to pleasure is suffering.

Freud first combined the two elements of pleasure and pain into a single dichotomous entity (sadomasochism), along the lines of Nietzsche's Apollonian-Dionysian dualism (reason vs passion) and most recently, neuroscientists confirmed pain *biologically* builds pleasure. The workout pain we feel in our body is a catalyst for us to change and grow, like a life-long gym session.

Nietzsche, a wise man himself, famously remarked that what does not kill us, makes us stronger. Suffering can make us more resilient, better able to endure hardships. Just as a muscle, in order to build up, must endure some pain, so our emotions must endure pain in order to strengthen.

From the implication of pleasure and pain as natural emotions on a continuum, art ultimately acquired a powerful value, in this human torment: "the instrument that allows us to momentarily reach the *noluntas*, that is, the liberation from the domain of the desires", be it Beauty or Sublime.

# Art Interpretation and Intention

---

What relevance, if any, do an artist's intentions have for our understanding of their work?

---

Principles of aesthetic judgment (and philosophy of mind) inevitably breed thinking of aesthetic appreciation - a philosophical account of the nature and value of art.

In Gothic architecture, light was considered the most beautiful revelation of God, which was heralded in its design.
*Rayonnant rose window in Notre Dame de Paris*

All along, artists have recreated reality, inducing the notion that works of art have meaning that requires interpretation:

"Beauty is not essential to Art, but meaning is."

In the Palaeolithic, art is action, in Egypt creative activity is the representation of what is known, in classical Greece art is mimesis or verisimilitude to the world and with the Romans, artworks become the narration of a story.

In the Middle Ages, art sets in as expression of inner feelings and emotions, whilst succumbing to a strong religious influence permeating the concepts of beauty and ugliness, with respect to God.

Nevertheless, art is no longer a manual activity to describe what one sees, more readily an intellectual activity that allows the knowledge of things.

In the sixteenth century, art is manifestation of what lies behind human reason, whereas across Romanticism artistry is the representation of what is unknown.

In nineteenth-century realism, artworks search for truth and reality is being represented just as artist's perception (Impressionism) or conforming to artist's sentiment (Expressionism). Art navigates peaks such as the overcoming of the limit in the Baroque and the nostalgic exaltation of a traditional beauty in Neoclassicism.

All this crash course on history of art testifies how artistic works have always been the subject of value judgments, for they were components of a cultural heritage that required particular attention from society, interested in preserving and passing them on, but also in destroying or replacing them.

In the present condition of culture, criticism ("the Art of interpreting Art", as the very first art critic Jonathan Richardson put it) is necessary for the production and affirmation of art and legitimizes the hypothesis of a sort of incompleteness or, at least, of a non-immediate communicability of the work of Art.

Banking on this, criticism proposes to fulfill a mediating function, between artists and the public: producers and users of artistic values.

Particularly after the Second Industrial revolution, the mediation turned into all the more necessary. Art need reach the whole of society, a large part of which is still denied access to, due to the socio-economical restructuring.

Consequently, art criticism aims to offer works of art a "just" or even scientific interpretation that would apply to everyone, without distinction of classes.

As an interpretative process and a type of artistic literature, art criticism had its baptism in the sixteenth century. The analytical practice broadly articulated into aesthetic interpretations about the work of art, or about the artist himself.

In the 20th century, the problem of interpretation transferred from aesthetics to literary theory (and semiotics), giving rise to the double question of recognizing the true meaning of the work of art and, pari passu, of the type of role to be attributed to the recipient.

The most traditional solution is objectivist (or essentialist) hermeneutics, convinced that in every text, the *intentio auctoris* is always unequivocally identifiable, that is, the meaning of a work is exactly what the author intended to attribute it.

This position, typical of both author-oriented criticism and structuralist semiotics, reveals different shades:

- the idea that the meaning is made definitive by the communion of the interpreter with the intention of the author (intuitionism);
- the conviction that it is, instead, the perfect knowledge of linguistic rules and norms that guarantees this finality (positivism);
- the position of someone like Hirsch (1983) who distinguished the objective and always discernible meaning of a text (meaning) from the value it assumes, *hic et nunc*, for the interpreter (significance).

Opposite to this first answer is the one proposed by perspectivism, who figure that the fulcrum of every interpretative process is the *intentio lectoris*: the meaning of a text does not coincide with the intentions of whoever produced it, but must be accepted as the result of interpreter's activity. Even this position - made known in the literary field as Reader-oriented criticism - has variations.

The most accredited today are those of Richard Rorty's pragmatism and Jonathan Culler's deconstructionism. For Rorty (1986) the interpretation of a text consists in the uses that the reader actually makes of it.

Going back to the author's intentionality is, for most, the correct path of criticism but the concept of *intentional fallacy* (Wimsatt & Beardsley, 1946) insinuated that the original meaning of the author is, perhaps, not the most important (or correct) interpretation of a work of art.

In a nutshell, there should be freedom of the public (audience reception) in determining what a text can say; a work of art, in sooth, is subject to a myriad of perspectives (*"the death of the author"*, according to Roland Barthes), particularly, in a different period of time than when it was created (i.e. when the work becomes *literature*).

Kant, as much as Diderot, in the articulation of the possibility of enjoying a work of art [taste] singled it out from the *genius* who is the creator of the work.

The Kantian differentiation almost completely disappeared nowadays, where the interpreter of the work of art, in a certain way, is also the one who recreates it.

Supporting that "books are like a picnic: the author brings the words and the reader the meaning" (Fyre), nevertheless rules out the case of anonymous or pseudonymous works.

To the rescue of this, the polysemous and polyvalent concept of *intentio operis* makes room for an interpretation beyond the author and the reader (Umberto Eco, *The Limits of Interpretation*, 1990), at the intersection between the rigid closure of objectivism and the indefinite opening of perspectivism.

The author creates the work whose meaning goes besides its intention (autonomous) and the recipients can never fully reach it (there is a *surplus*), so they find fill-in references to their own, limited system of signs (decoding).

The philosophy of aesthetic interpretation nurtures a philosophy of language, whose misunderstandings [aberrant decodings] eventually determine the success or failure of a communication, prominently the aesthetic one.

With the complications of conceptual art, the avant-garde artist became *provoc-auteur* and post-modernism exasperated the confusion on the search for meaning, with irony and vagueness. Arthur Danto drew the inference in 1997:

"All there is at the end is theory, Art having finally become vaporized in a dazzle of pure thought about itself, and remaining, as it were, solely as the object of its own theoretical consciousness."

Thus, art appears to have progressively paralyzed itself by overanalyzing its nature and hinge on continuous narrative.

The aim of the history of the world (and therefore, the history of art), since Hegel, has been that the spirit [its Idea] reaches the knowledge of what it really is to objectify such knowledge, fulfilling itself and practically manifesting itself. However, a teleological view of art, in these terms, has waxed into an obstacle to its very existence.

## DID YOU KNOW?

Extremely tall platform shoes (*"chopines"*) were all the rage in Venice in the 16th and 17th centuries, as they helped women walk through the muddy streets, without getting their dresses dirty. It was hard to walk and wearers needed a servant to help them balance.

Domenico Scarlatti composed his "Cat's Fugue" after his cat, *Pulcinella*, walked across his keyboard. Haydn didn't like people falling asleep during his concerts, so he wrote the *Surprise Symphony*: quiet and relaxing until the end, when the music gets louder and ends with a bang.

The history of cosmetic spans at least 6000 years. Some historians can even date back to the African Middle Stone Age 100,000 years ago, where they used red mineral pigments on their face.

# CHAPTER XI

# Religion

## *Existence and Attributes of God*

---

Is there a persuasive argument for the existence of God or divine design?

---

Human positions on the existence or non-existence of God can be schematically divided into three major strands: theistic, atheist and agnostic.

For theism, there are sufficient reasons to believe in the existence of God or divinity; for atheism, there are either no sufficient or necessary premises to affirm the existence of God and divinity, looked on as impossible from the rational or ontological standpoint; lastly, agnosticism feels God is unknowable, at least currently.

Within theism, naives can spot monotheism, pantheism and deism. Theism and atheism feuded with mostly logical-dialectical attitudes until the 19th century, stretching as far as the supernatural domain, by now. Both fields branch out, in turn, based on the thesis that one's position is, or is not, definitively demonstrated by the arguments.

In the West, the term God typically refers to the monotheistic concept of a Supreme Being, whence we cannot conceive anything greater than, or in Anselm of Canterbury's legendary maxim:

> *"Deus est ens quo nihil maius cogitari potest"*
> PROSLOGION, 1077

The Medieval Catholic theologian elaborated the ontological proof for the existence of God, *a priori*, that is, the argument is true, without the aid of empirical validity - it is a truth of reason, purely rational. From the awareness that God does not have the same ontological nature as an entity - "being pure being" - Anselm asks the *insipiens* (whoever does not know) what they can think of anything greater, whose idea lacks nothing.

Perfect and infinite ideas cannot exist in the mind of a finite, and imperfect human being, thus must necessarily born out of an Other (which corresponds with God).

The French Benedictine monk Gaunilo, whilst not questioning the existence of God, contested the *a priori* proof in his *Liber Pro Insipiente*. From his angle, people cannot ground the existence of God on thought, in order to warrant its existence in the sensible reality, for impossible things can also be thought.

It follows that Anselm's definition of divinity is either deduced from something else (e.g. revelation, therefore it is not *a priori* proof) or it is completely arbitrary and as such, the problem of the very possibility of "thinking about the definition" sets in.

In a parody, Gaunilo further objected that "if I think of a very perfect island, it does not mean that it also exists in reality".

Anselm defended his approach by arguing that God and an island shall not be on the same level, since his proof was applicable only to maximum perfection.

Side to side, the ontological proof is reworked by Descartes in his *Meditations*.

The French philosopher gathered that the ideas in our mind are always the effect of a cause, which may come from the outside, from within us or be innate (out of an infinite power): God is the sum of all perfections, whose concept is innate in the human intellect and unreproducible alone, as the notion of actual infinity.

In other words, thinking of a most perfect God lacking the attribute of existence is contradictory, an interpretation reduced in a purely logical way by Leibniz, later on with the maxim: "if God is possible, he necessarily exists" (1701).

NASA's illustration of the Gamma-ray bubbles from Sgr A*, the supermassive black hole at the Galactic Center of the Milky Way. The Central Sun (6th Cosmic Plane), which is the invisible source of all that is in our Solar System (7th Cosmic Plane).

Thomas Aquinas, in his *Summa Theologiae*, declared that God exists and can be proved in Five Ways.

The first and most evident way is inferred from motion (*Ex Motu*): everything that moves is moved by another and everyone recognizes that it is God.

The second route applies the *principle of efficient cause* (*Ex Causa*): it is necessary to admit a first efficient cause, which everyone calls God.

The third way depends on the possible (or *contingent*) and on the *necessary* (*Ex Contingentia*): it is inevitable to admit the existence of a necessary Being, who does not derive his own necessity from others but causes necessity in others (that is, a creator Being); everyone recognizes that it is God.

The fourth way reckons the degrees found in things (*Ex gradu Perfectionis*): what is the cause of being for all contingent entities (supreme entity) is, consequently, also the most perfect (*summum bonum*), which everyone calls God.

The fifth modus shapes from the government of things (*Ex fine*): to achieve perfection, every being tends to an end, ordered by an intelligent Being (teleological thesis), which everyone calls God.

Aquinas's proofs generally proceed from effects to cause, with a similar structure. They draw from different sources: Plato and Aristotle (who first formulated categories of "power" and "act", with a proof of the Motionless Being), Neoplatonic thought (as regards to the degrees of perfection), Avicenna and some Muslim thinkers (who first stressed the difference between *being contingent* and *being necessary*).

The main counterargument is that these notions use infinite regress. Nonetheless, similar structure is found in Zeno's paradoxes, which were resolved centuries later, proving that infinite regress is not contradictory and is logically admissible.

Deductive arguments for the existence of God start with formally logical premises to reach affirmative conclusions on ontological levels; basically, existence is admitted, so as not to break the principle of non-contradiction (*reductio ad absurdum*). The leap from the logical possibility to the necessity of existence occurs whenever any other hypothesis, which denies the existence of God becomes logically impossible.

Gödel's ontological proof and mathematical trials fall into this category. The mathematician supplied a logical verification for the existence of God: God is a Being who resolves within the positive qualities of all real entities and must necessarily exist, as the foundation of the mathematical universe order.

The *Gödelian proof*, which flows from five axioms and hinges on a rigid formal theorem, is based on the premise that it would not be logically plausible to admit the possibility of a single Being provided with all "positive properties", including existence itself, without attributing to the latter an actual reality; otherwise this would be a mathematical contradiction in terms.

On the other end, inductive arguments sponsor that logic, science, ethics and other phenomena display a fairly high probability for the existence of God (*transcendental coherence*), as they make no sense without, when "they are considered in a naturalistic rather than theistic setting" (*The Foundations of Beliefs*, Arthur Balfour, 1895).

Nonetheless, a great deal of obscure points still beg the question.

According to Kant, St. Anselm's proof for the existence of God made a fundamental error, that is, it makes a leap from a logical to an ontological level. It does nothing but demonstrate the concept of existence, yet not existence itself.

To argue that a *first motionless engine* must logically exist, as Aquinas did, does not mean that such first motionless engine really exists. As a result, philosophy made necessary to reopen discussions to determine *a posteriori* proofs for the existence of God.

Empirical arguments in favour of the existence of God make use of definitions and axioms: the *anthropic argument*, for instance, uses basic facts to prove God, namely our existence. The temporal lobe has been of interest by neurosciences, so much so it has been termed the "God center" of the brain.

The cosmological argument hails from our experience and from there, offshoots the existence of God as the cause of what exists (world).

Here, critics find again two main errors:

1. the *cause principle*, deduced from the sensible world is valid only for the sensible world and cannot give origin to a synthetic judgment beyond the sphere of experience;
2. the cosmological proof partially re-proposes the ontological paradox, in fact, once it has been established that the supreme Being [God] is a condition of the world, its existence is yet to be proved anyway.

The physical-theological argument counteracts from the order, variety and beauty of the world to go back to God, as the ultimate and supreme Being above all perfection (ultimate cause).

Fault-finders of the cosmological proof also patrol here, as the line of reasoning, at best, is for the existence of an 'architect of the world' but not of a creator, whose idea everything is subjected to. To prove this, the physical-theological criterion depends on the cosmological one, which in turn retains the ontological problem.

The moral argument is the most persuasive, to date and holds that objective morality exists, therefore, God exists. For Kant, God represents a *practical* moral ideal, whose existence is assumed and where all moral thought takes root (postulate of practical reason).

Quidem, it is common for religions to have value frameworks regarding personal behaviour meant to guide adherents in discerning right and wrong. These encompass the Triple Gems of Jainism, Islam's Sharia, Catholicism's Catechism, Buddhism's Noble Eightfold Path, and Zoroastrianism's "good thoughts, good words, and good deeds" concept, among others.

As *ought implies can*, common objections to Kant's logic noted the issue of *entailment*: the perfect good, as well as any moral action is deemed possible, yet not actually attainable (Everitt, 2003).

The argument for morality, formulated by John Locke and by contemporaries such as Mackie, often pivots on a syllogism, whereby objective moral truths exist and conscience is the evidence. The same concept was supported in Germany, by theologian Friedrich Schleiermacher, who called attention to "an internal religious sense we feel religious truths through". Manifestly, religion consists only of internal perception and dogmatic doctrines are not essential.

Over and beyond the aspect of surrender associated with faith, belief in the existence of God is seemingly an effect of the miracle - an extraordinary event ascribed to divine agency - because prodigy engenders faith in the souls of those who are its recipients or witnesses.

The seventieth and last miracle recognized by the Church is the healing of a nun, Sister Bernadette Moriau. Of the seven thousand healings attributed to Our Lady of Lourdes, over two thousand have been recognized as inexplicable and of these, only seventy have been formally recognized as proven miraculous occurences.

A critical investigation into the founders of major religious groups respectively Jesus, Mohammed and Buddha, burgeoned at the outset of the century in the quest to erode the obvious mythical contents of religions and achieve a fact-based, historical reconstruction of its role models.

The theological problem about the real existence of Jesus of Nazareth, commonly regarded as the Incarnation of God persists today.

On the one side, defenders of the historicity of Jesus rely on the writings of historians like Tacitus, the correspondences of Pliny the

Younger with Trajan or Josephus Flavius, who chronicled about Jesus around the middle of the 1st century. The opposition instead uphold the theory that Jesus never existed (the myth of Jesus) on the basis that there is no written evidence, historical records such as the census, to prove its existence.

This should not come as a surprise in view of the fact that the sources available on the work of the leaders of religions have been set down, almost entirely, by the circle of followers.

The life of Jesus, by way of illustration - effectively summed up by the Catholic biblical scholar John Paul Meier as that of a "marginal Jew" - was not that important as to attract the attention of the historian or scholar of the time, rather only that of faithful people, over time. There is no certainty about Muhammad either, as regards to the date of birth or death. What is reported by Islam simply constitutes the opinion of a relative, albeit substantial, majority of traditionalists and faithful.

Anonymous illustration of al-Bīrūnī's The Remaining Signs of Past Centuries, depicting Muhammad prohibiting Nasīʾ during the Farewell Pilgrimage, 17th-century Ottoman copy of a 14th-century (Ilkhanate) manuscript

Many modern Protestant theologians follow in Schleiermacher's footsteps, and teach that the existence of God cannot be proved; the certainty of this gospel truth is provided only by our inner experience, feelings and perception.

Modernist Christianity also denies the demonstrable existence of God.

According to Kierkegaard, the very term 'existence' applied to God is inadequate.

The Christian philosopher declared that "faith is a paradox (not the absurd or the irrational)" and promoted that "God must be accepted by faith and that's all - God shall not be explained".

Faith is therefore a risk, for it requires personal adherence to surmise, statements that objectively do not present any guarantee and are in stark contrast to the normal criteria of truth.

# Soul and Immortality

> If God cannot change, then there is a limit to God, therefore God does not exist.

A vexed problem endogenous to the existence of God is that traditional beliefs usually attribute deities various *supernatural powers*. God's supernatural abilities, in fact, are frequently tabled in lieu of the inability of empirical methods to establish its existence.

In Karl Popper's philosophy of science, the assertion of a supernatural God existence is a hypothesis that cannot be falsified, therefore, close to scientific investigation.

One strategy to corroborate the validity of any argument regarding the existence of God is to generally examine divine characteristics and then delve into specifics for each religion, faith or belief.

Different theologies and Holy Books have different narratives of God. To cite an instance, in Christianity, God is regularly seen as a loving and merciful father figure, while in Judaism, God is generally viewed as the all-powerful creator of the universe. In Islam, God is often seen as a merciful and compassionate Being who carefully judges human actions.

The role of prophets and messengers also differ: in Islam, prophets are considered to be messengers of God, who were sent to guide humanity and impart divine teachings. In Christianity, Jesus is seen as the ultimate messenger of God, who came to Earth as a sacrifice for humanity's sins.

In Hinduism, the concept of reincarnation is recurring, the soul will be reborn after death (karma). In Christianity, the belief in heaven and hell is central; individuals will be judged based on their actions during their lifetime, *cupio dissolvi*.

*Holy Trinity (1756–1758) by Szymon Czechowicz, showing God the Father, God the Son, and the Holy Spirit, all of whom are revered in Christianity as a single deity*

Religious practices and rituals also justify pluralism about God in theology. In Islam, the five daily prayers, fasting during Ramadan and performing pilgrimage to Mecca are all considered essential customs.

In Hinduism, performing *puja*, visiting temples and following a vegetarian diet are common religious routines.

Holy Books are deemed to be the divine revelations of God that serve as lighthouses for religious practice, and belief. Different Holy Books, however, play different roles in their respective theologies. To make clear, the Quran is considered to be the literal word of God in Islam, while the Bible is seen as divinely inspired but not necessarily the literal word of God in Christianity.

A common monotheistic definition holds that God possesses all possible perfection with qualities such as omniscience, omnipotence and perfect benevolence. However, this implication is problematic.

Epicurus is generally known as the prime critic, with the problem of evil, sometimes called *"the Epicurean Paradox"* or *"the riddle of Epicurus"*.

In Western theology and philosophy of religion, the problem of evil stems from the urgency to explain the paradox of evil when it is believed that there is a divinity that is considered good, omnipotent and omniscient.

The case argues for the logical problem of evil, that is all the kinds, quantities and distributions of evil in the world may imply the non-existence of God, to some extent. The evidential version of the problem of evil (also known as the probabilistic or inductive version) counts against or lowers the probability of the truth of theism, even if it were logically consistent with the existence of God.

Consequently, the evidence of wickedness in the world would depend on plausible (and not hidden) reasons for God's permission for profound immorality, leading to embrace *distheism*, the belief that God exists, but is not completely good.

Theodicy (or *"problem of God's justice"*) along the logical and evidential arguments of evil contest the existence of a God who is both omnipotent and omnibenevolent, insisting that this first uncaused cause, supreme perfect Being would not allow the existence of perceptible pain or suffering, which can be easily pinpointed, as we speak.

This is also notable as *moral argument*: if God existed, it would be *non-moral* from the point of view of human understanding, therefore useless as a reference.

The polemic is not strictly about the existence of any deity, so it is also supported by theists and other groups as well as by atheists. Furthermore, since God is infinite, by such very nature, divinity should contain evil within, a principle that clashes with the dogma whereby "only good proceeds from God without the slightest presence of evil in it".

Deists contest this, by conceiving evil as the absence of good, which is precisely the essence of God.

The *argument from poor design* disputes the tenet that a God created the world, on account of that life forms exhibit poor or malevolent traits, which can be easily explained in evolutionary or naturalistic terms.

The *argument from nonbelief* disputes the existence of an almighty God who wants humans to believe in him, stating that such a God would do a better job in gathering believers.

This debate is challenged by the claim that God aims to test human beings to see who has more faith, yet is rejected by the *paradox of free will*: it makes no sense that God tests us, as being omniscient implies knowledge of how this turns out and as a result, it irreversibly undermines the concept of free will.

The paradox of omnipotence and other theological versions (*"Could God create a stone so heavy that could not lift?"*) are one of the many anomalies attesting that the definitions or descriptions of a God are logically contradictory, thus disallow its formulation applied to the nature of God and conclude that God is either *accidentally omnipotent* or more easily, *non-omnipotent*.

Holy Trinity (1756–1758) by Szymon Czechowicz, showing God the Father, God the Son, and the Holy Spirit, all of whom are revered in Christianity as a single deity

Hence, the *transcendental argument for the non-existence of God* gainsays the existence of an intelligent creator, showing that such a being would make logic and morals dependent, which is incompatible with the presuppositional assertion that these are necessary, therefore it contradicts the efficacy of science. The puzzle seeks to generalize this proof to all necessary features of the universe, to all views of God.

A notable reflection counteracted that due to humankind's poor knowledge, human beings cannot claim to understand God or the ultimate plan, at all (*argumentum ad ignorantiam*).

To simplify good and bad, and the God dilemma, Eastern philosophies controversially posited that evil, such as suffering and diseases, is an illusion.

Concepts such as the Taoist *yin and yang* further suggest that evil and good are complementary opposites within a whole: if one disappears, the other must also disappear, so evil does not really occur, except as a comparison to God.

But even if one were to suppose, with a more lenient approach to the enigma, that there is no best of all possible worlds (Leibniz), the possibility of evil is clearly not addressed.

Logical positivists like Rudolf Carnap and A. J. Ayer, see any discussion of divinities as outright nonsense.

For neo-empiricists and adherents to similar schools of thought, statements about religion or other transcendental attributes cannot have a truth value and are regarded as meaningless.

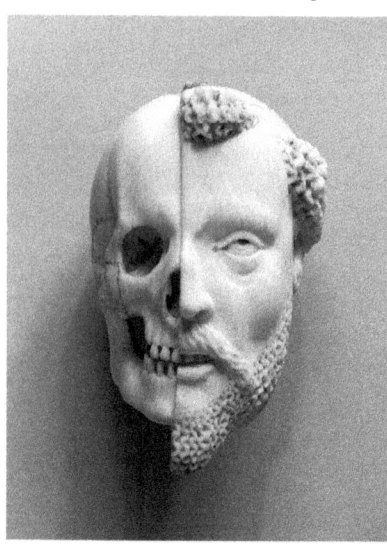

16th-/17th-century ivory pendant, Monk and Death, recalling mortality and the certainty of death (Walters Art Museum)

The lion's share of theological answers to this, coming from the Judeo-Christian culture, is that the world is corrupt because of the sin of the human race (the *Original Sin*).

Due to the sin, the world has fallen from God's grace and it is now imperfect, that is why evil and suffering persist.

A consequent defence is the *theodicy of the afterlife*, whereby the joys of heaven will compensate for suffering on Earth.

There is the *credo* that when we suffer from evil, it is always because of an evil we ourselves have previously done (Karma).

Skeptics ponder that if any theodicy were true, it would defeat morality altogether. In layman's terms, all evil events, including human actions, would be rationalized as permitted or affected by God and if every conceivable state of affairs is compatible with God's "goodness", the concept becomes meaningless.

Devils are evil and immoral sovereign deities, hated and feared by humankind. As religious dogmas stand, they are ancient and very powerful, always aligned with temptation and the spread of sin. To sin means to violate a moral precept; for a believer, breaking a commandment from God.

More than 1 billion people in the world look up to Mecca as a spiritual guide and more than 2 billion followers consider the Vatican as the compass according to whom to behave and differentiate good from evil.

Human sins have equally triggered a long record of bribery and scandal in religions, which have grown into unscrupulous enterprises ready to do anything to stay afloat.

Six thousand years of religious history tell of the heart of Judaism, Islam and Christianity as a place that is simultaneously also the heart of trades, privileges and distortions irreconcilable with the promoted doctrine itself.

Perhaps many of us are not aware of it, but these religions are, first of all, *absolute theocratic monarchies*: an absolutist state where a single man, the monarch - be it the Pope, Caliph or the Chief Rabbi - decides and governs without any democratic control by any institution, since they believe to be invested with such power directly by a God.

What makes the background of these religious faiths evil are the characters, being priests, leaders or messengers of Messiah, and the place where the horrible events took place: the Church, Mosques, synagogues, the Holy Land.

Needless to mention the murders, illegitimate children and sale of ecclesiastical offices that characterized the medieval period of Christian history, the silence of the Vatican on the Holocaust and the torments of Pope Paul VI who premeditated in his encyclicals how the Church was shaken by the *"smoke of Satan"* within its walls.

The interests of the Holy See have routinely proved to be non-transparent and directed towards values distant from charity, equality, peace, goodness, self-control.

In the 1990s, a great deal of financial and political scandals uncovered how the Vatican Bank and its relations with the mafia, masquerade money laundering with fictitious charitable associations and foundations; leaked Vatican documents, in late 2012, exposed the blackmailing of homosexual clergy by individuals outside the Church and most recently, in 2018, a former Bank-head $62 million embezzlement, using a real estate scam in London.

With the Roman Catholic Church weathering one case after another of priests who sexually abused boys, donations collected for sick children are reportedly used instead to offset the costs of Cardinals' mega penthouses and properties in Rome.

The Catholic Church expresses clear opposition to any public recognition of unions between people of the same sex or gender transition which is, for some critics, evidence of ideological homophobia and transphobia in the Catholic tradition.

Homosexual orientation, which many men and women present, is recognized by the catechism as a "disordered inclination" or in any case, as a sin forbidden by God.

When Pope Francis condemned laws criminalizing homosexuality, many misinterpreted the Catholic Church's sympathetic call for redemption as inclusion - his full remarks were "it is not a crime, but only a sin".

Pope Francis only paraphrased the idea, shared by all Abrahamic religions, that homosexuals are sinners to be welcomed, like a sick or a divorced person, and as such, they are obliged to chastity, prayer and sacramental grace, so as to resolutely approach Christian perfection.

God's solution to our sin is always personal sacrifice, the zenith of evil purification. With this in mind, the Catholic Church's tolerance towards gay clergy or mercifulness over its "homosexual subculture" suddenly makes sense: choosing priesthood to expiate the sin of homosexuality, debauchery or gender transition is the greatest accomplishment of personal sacrifice, an excellent purpose that encourages ecclesiastical forgiveness.

Along the Catholic style and despite Jewish religious doctrine subsists on nonviolence, respect, truth and peaceful containments, Judaism concretely translated into orthodox intolerance for diversity, unconcerned citizenship and fanaticism against modernity driven by the concept of *chosenness* - what Paul the Apostle firstly defined as self-made righteousness (ethnic pride) - whose effects include but are not limited to Tel Aviv shootings against LGBT people, circumcision ritual of infant males (brit milah), fundamentalist warfare and kosher slaughter.

The gathering of the Jewish diaspora in the land of Israel became the core mission behind Israel's practices in its occupation of the Palestinian territories, the source of one of the world's most enduring conflicts, ongoing since 1948: the Israeli-Palestinian conflict.

Jewish claim Jerusalem as the capital of Israel, the world's only Jewish state where to gather all the exiles, according to the Sacred Scriptures.

Hand on heart, the status of Jerusalem and the Israeli state is disputable. USA-whipped, Western diplomatic practice only supported the creation of a Jewish homeland in 1948, primarily as a sop for Holocaust collective guilt and under the guise of democratization, for the United States to gain territory control and proximity to harsh Asian competitors, on behalf of economic interests, Westernization and strategic risk reduction.

Up until the Reformation, artists almost exclusively depicted religious subjects. Works of art were often commissioned by powerful members of the Church, or to grain the Church's favour, so the subject matter of important religious paintings and sculptures is religious, in nature.

Eradicating religion is impossible, because it would also mean to wipe out the mural of *The Last Supper* by Leonardo da Vinci in Milan's Saint Mary of Grace convent, Michelangelo's *Sistine Chapel* or Raphael Rooms in the Vatican, Pinturicchio's frescoes in Siena Cathedral and Vatican Library or Masaccio's particulars of the Brancaccio Chapel in Florence, to name but a few.

Religion is not just faith but indelible cultural and historical identity, even influencing how people dress like Hasidic Jews or Islamic women typify.

History (and art) is the foremost expression of a nation and its unique geneaology, that is why even atheists or infidels preserve religious enterprises, willy-nilly.

Unfortunately, homogenization of countries around the world or *Americanization* has transfigured worldwide diversity, deliberately threatening the cultural identity of nations, in primis the traditionalism of Middle East.

The widespread globalization belief in the universality of the West's values and political systems, perceived as ongoing cultural imperialism only invigorates differences and antagonizes civilizations (the *Clash of Civilizations*, from the eponymous book, 1996).

From a sharper angle, Samuel P. Huntington declared the West as naive as reluctant to accept that people's religious identities would be the primary source of conflict, in post-Cold war period, simply because this ideology of globalizing the West built the international system, wrote its laws, and gave it substance in the form of the United Nations.

According to Bruno Bauer, a 19-century philosopher and denier of the historical existence of Jesus, the demands of religion are incompatible with the idea of human rights. True human emancipation requires a secular state that leaves no room for social identities like religion.

Certainly religion is not the root of evil, for as Karl Marx later highlighted in his essay *"On the Jewish Question"* in response to the debate, individuals may be spiritually and politically free in a secular state, yet still be deprived of freedom due to economic inequality - an assumption that would later form the basis of his criticism on capitalism.

Desolation and ruin alike also characterize the current state of the Arab world, a world where religion is equally politicized and politics sanctified.

Many know little to nothing about the vast role played by Arab and Muslim slavers in the African slave, the longest slave trade in history.

The sale of African slaves became popular in the seventh century when Islam was gaining strength in North Africa - seven centuries before Europeans explored the continent and ten centuries before West Africans were sold across the Atlantic to America.

Over several centuries countless East Africans were sold as slaves by Muslim Arabs to the Middle East, and other places via the Sahara desert, also known as the trans-Saharan trade or Eastern slave trade.

We all know the folly of Islamic terrorism responsible for the massacres of innocent peoples, and we appreciated their hatred for individual liberties over the last thirty years, strongly juxtaposing terrorist acts, on a global scale, to the professed Islamic values of *Salam*, kindness, justice, respect.

Financially powerful, fundamentalist, militant and nationalist organizations from the Arab League such as Al Qa'ida, Hamas, the Taliban, Boko Haram flaunt a barbarism that surpasses all imagination.

Deeply ingrained religious motivations include an overriding will to restore the Caliphate as a pan-Islamic state (ISIS) by establishing sharia law and allegedly purify Islam, to obtain the Islamic glory and heavenly rewards of martyrdom, to fight for the supremacy of Islam over all other religions and gain retribution by the armed *jihad* for the perceived injustices of unbelievers against Muslims.

The atavic, political anger with the State of Israel in the Muslim world provides Islamic terrorists with a significant reason to terrorist activity, and self-determination to pursue the ongoing military, and political Israeli–Palestinian conflict for the sovereignty over Palestine, or the "liberation of Palestine" and recognition of a Palestinian state - either in place of both Israel and the Palestinian territories or solely in the Palestinian territories.

Israel is heavily attacked by Arabs for ethnical cleansing, for continuing to exercise apartheid in Palestine and so is the West, for legitimizing their theft of land.

Antisemitic tropes about Jewish wealth have been around for centuries and conspiracy theories are a prevalent feature of Arab culture, and politics - a metropolitan *maladie*, which is often referred to in Arab media as "the War against Islam".

Primitive, uneducated *islamophilia* brings Islam into disrepute, because *historia lux veritatis*, Jews fled as refugees after suffering prosecution from Arab lands, and deadly programs like the Farhud of Baghdad in 1941.

> "1.5 million Arabs in Israel - whatever challenge they face - enjoy full rights to vote and to be elected in the Knesset, they work as doctors or lawyers, they serve on the Supreme Court. Now I'd like to ask the members of Arab states: how many Jews live in your countries? How many Jews lived in Egypt, Iraq, Kuwait, Lebanon, Lybia, Morocco? Once upon a time the Middle East was full of Jews. Algeria had a 140,000 Jews, Algeria where are your Jews? Egypt used to have 75,000 Jews, Egypt where are your Jews? Syria, you had tens of thousands of Jews, where are your Jews? Iraq, you had over 130,000 Jews, where are your Jews? [...] Mr. President, where is the real apartheid?
>
> **U.N. WATCH'S *HILLEL NEUER* SILENCES UNITED NATIONS, 2017**

In the name of threatened nationalism or purity the worst crimes are committed: suicide attacks, filmed rapes, hijackings whose most infamous were the "9/11" attacks that killed nearly 3,000 people on a single day in 2001, looting, the sale of women, the destruction of archaeological and historical sites, kidnappings, killings and live streamed executions, with the Charlie Hebdo shooting in 2015 or this autumn's Hamas attack in Israel being the deadliest in a series conducted by violent non-state actors.

Religious belief in its own authenticity is a theological self-conception, not a historical reality. The sacred texts are not the unchanging repositories of wisdom their believers assume them to be. Today, an impressive accumulation of evidence shows how far religions have gone to make their textual legacy consistent with their present culture: they have changed or censored enough to reflect the needs of the religious authorities.

Scholarship has been ever so important, in part to discover the religion's own success at covering up inconvenient aspects of their past, through exegesis, synods or public commentaries. This is how numerous versions of monotheistic belief have always been possible, even within a motley framework and quite frankly, this is why religions are still on the rise, with heavy fanaticism, after centuries of crimes.

The most striking facet of this breakthrough is certainly that all religions boast so much about fighting evil for good but do not realize how they are, single-handedly, the main cause of evil and human cruelty: they generate violence, confrontation, wars and death, in every part of the world more than money. As Andrew White quipped:

> "Ritualized killing is performed in hopes of earning the favour of supernatural forces."

From those facts, it is necessary to face the issue of violence and hypocrisy as constitutive aspects of religions and, moving on to the present time, to recognize how religious faith is the source of humankind's most dramatic events and deadliest atrocities: the Crusades, the Taiping Rebellion, the failure of the Arab Spring, the terrorist attacks, the war in Iraq and Afghanistan, the Atlantic slave trade, to randomly name but a few.

Should we intend, not so much to solve, but at least to face the knot of "religious violence" as well as the other evils deriving from faiths, we must first of all recognize that religions - all of them - are fallible and incomplete expressions, and there is a "beyond" that no religious caste possesses, and no dogma fully expresses.

In short, to overcome violence and the evil, every religion must accept to get over itself, with a radical effort of philosophical self-criticism.

The theological void of absolute opposition to an Anti-Christ led 19th century classical philologist and cultural critic prodigy Friedrich Nietzsche to a direct confrontation with religion, with the well-known thesis of the *"death of God"*.

Nietzsche's work became notable for a violent destructive criticism of the past, represented by the moral and religious tradition of the West, and his passionate appeal to the future, with the creation of a new human capable of facing the tragic nature of life, without the need for philosophical or religious certainties.

God is supposed to be eternal, and thus cannot die. Nietzsche's claim, however, is that "God" is a fiction created by human beings. Thus, God "dies" when there is no good reason to believe that God exists.

The death of God is a liberation for the human spirit and people have the opportunity to create their values, and live according to them.

The German philosopher came to the conclusion that religions spread an ethical principle throughout the world (the need for truth, truthfulness, sincerity), which ultimately turned against them.

The principle reveals how Christianity is the fruit of a judgmental attitude towards life, of resentment and of the opposition of a "world behind the world" to the reality of this world we live in; all the virtues preached by Christianity are pseudo-virtues and have led to an ever more radical rejection of life.

In modern world, *"God is dead. God remains dead. And we have killed him"*, no longer able to stimulate the inventiveness of humankind, to guide their lives and to provoke the discovery of new values, but stands as an obstacle to any form of renewal.

The Nietzschean notion of God's death, therefore, appears very different from any form of traditional atheism, secularism or unbelief in God; it is rather the conclusion of an overall historical-cultural evaluation which is expressed in the nihilistic diagnosis of the Greek-Jewish-Christian civilization, and preponderant moral assumptions in Europe.

In the end, Nietzsche argued for a "revaluation of values", because little by little, the "real world" became a fairy tale and the inconsistency of the theological conception of truth came ever more to light.

Christianity is viewed as "Platonism for the people", in the sense that religion affirms two realities and opposes the values of heaven (the idea of immortality, the existence of an otherworld) to those of the Earth. Thus, religion is for the weak, the defeated ones.

This work clearly opposes the pagan principle of force to the Christian principle of love, the aristocratic principle of the superhuman to the democratic principle of equality, the optimistic principle of vital joy to the pessimistic principle of pain, the voluntarist instinct to the rationalistic principle of autonomy, the republicans to the democrats.

> "God is dead. God remains dead. And we have killed him. How shall we comfort ourselves, the murderers of all murderers? What was holiest and mightiest of all that the world has invented for boredom has also bled to death under our knives for boredom: who will wipe this blood off our hands?"
>
> FRIEDRICH NIETZSCHE, *THE GAY SCIENCE*, SECTION 125

Secularity fleshed out from Christian history and Karl Marx characterised the world of exploitation with religion, as a form of protest. The socialist revolutionary elaborated on the idea that the function of religion is to relieve pain in life.

> "Religion is... a protest against real suffering. Religion is the sigh of the oppressed creature, the heart of a heartless world and the soul of soulless conditions. It is the opium of the people."

Others such as Talcott Parson and Emilie Durkheim hold that religion creates social solidarity, collective consciousness and social control between people. This emphasizes that religion plays a key role in society as a social institution.

Freud asserted that religion is a largely unconscious neurotic response to repression. By repression, the founder of psychoanalysis meant that civilized societies demand that we shall not fulfil all our desires immediately, rather that they have to be repressed.

By promising rewards in the next life, religion helps the poor bear their lot and privation in this one. Faith is sacrifice, hence religion thrives among low socio-economic classes, where privation of freedom, pride or basic desires is the bread and butter.

Gobsmacked by this, Nietzsche judges religion as "slave morality" created by the powerful upper class clerics to universalize the plight of the slave onto the humankind, through fatalistic, handcuffing religious principles like humility, charity and pity.

These engender pessimism, cynicism and apathy, thus hindering our social mobility and life affirmation.

Though rarely mentioned by modern historians, clergy in fact has formed an important part of the elites since the Middle Ages, also known as "First Estate" to remark their highest rank in the social hierarchy, even before nobility.

This is still the winning tactic and why religions essentially capitalize on resentment: the defining characteristic of the poor, who live indignant at the lack of utility compared to the rich, and whose only aspiration turns out to be slaving the masters, out of revenge, other than outperforming life.

Freedom is a threat to religions, because a call for personal self-discovery and self-overcoming could awaken "the will to power" in the faithful, and the slave could conquer the upper echelon. To avoid this, religion is necessary primarily or solely for the weak.

Those with a victim mentality, in fact, believe they have been the victim of wrongdoing by others or have otherwise suffered misfortune through no fault of their own.

The creator mindset, a cut above, prioritizes continuous learning, skill development, and by embracing challenges, leads people to personal growth and to take effective actions to achieve the life they want.

For, as life coaches would sell you in present times, when you accept personal responsibility or accountability, you believe that you create everything in your life, that you can be anything you want to be.

Albeit misunderstood by Nazism and complex to read through, Nietzsche stays ever so contemporary with his genealogical critique of religion. He was, deep down, a forerunner [guru] of contemporary motivational coaches and "lifestyle", as we know the concept today, intended as human action, health, individual identity or will to succeed, in vogue under the aegis of existential pain of today's society.

Max Müller (1823-1900) is known for being the founder of the scientific study of religion; he introduced a comparative method that became comparative religion.

Further, the sacred-profane dichotomy is a concept knitted by the French sociologist Émile Durkheim in *The Elementary Forms of Religious Life* (1995), who considered it to be the central characteristic of religion:

> "Religion is a unified system of beliefs and practices relative to *sacred things*, that is to say, things set apart and forbidden."

Durkheim explicitly stated that the sacred–profane dichotomy is not equivalent to good-evil, as the sacred could be either good or evil, and the profane could be either as well.

British anthropologist Jack Goody better puts it:

> "Many societies have no words that translate as sacred or profane and that ultimately, just like the distinction between natural and supernatural, it was very much a product of European religious thought rather than a universally applicable criterion."

For Tomolo Masuzawa, any cosmology without a sacred–profane binary was rendered invisible by the field of religious studies, privileging Christianity at the expense of non-Christian systems, because the binary was supposed to be "universal".

The profane world consists of all that people can know through their senses; it is the natural world of everyday life that people experience as either comprehensible or at least ultimately knowable — the *Lebenswelt* or lifeworld (Peter Berger, *A Rumour of Angels*, 1973*)*.

In contrast, the sacred, or *sacrum* in Latin, comprises all that exists beyond the everyday, natural world that people experience with their senses. As such, the sacred or numinous can inspire feelings of awe, owing to the fact that it is regarded as ultimately unknowable and beyond limited human abilities to perceive, and comprehend.

Durkheim pointed out though that there are degrees of sacredness, so that an amulet for example may be sacred yet little respected.

Influential agnostic Bible scholar Bart D. Ehrman, in 2008, observed that

> "The apocalyptic parts of the Bible, including the New Testament, see suffering as caused by evil cosmic forces, which God, for mysterious reasons, has allowed to act in the world, but which will soon be defeated and all will be restored".

Evil and suffering may be necessary for spiritual growth.

Recalling Schopenhauer's description of the will to live in denial and the subsequent empty nothingness, Nietzsche proclaims of God that "in him nothingness is deified and the will to nothingness is made holy!".

Moral goodness or love for God cannot be achieved if there is no evil and suffering in the world, hence the *epistemic distance* (John Hick, 1966).

## *Life after Death*

---

**In what way, if any, could you continue to exist after the death of your body?**

---

Philosophically speaking, being is something absolute and does not need anything else, whereas existence does not have 'being' in its own right; instead, it receives it from something else (*ex* means out of). Such subordinated tension toward absolute and transcendence designated human beings, since pre-history.

God is the concept of superior being, of a transcendental and / or immanent type, something "totally other" than what is ordinarily perceived, whose relationship with the human being (interpreted differently, according to the various types of creed) takes the name of religion.

A flower, a skull and an hourglass stand for life, death, and time in this 17th-century painting by Philippe de Champaigne

Throughout its adventures, philosophy has always faced the problem of the meaning and truth value of religion, seeking, in particular, to demonstrate the existence of divinity and to show its characters, and functions in relation to humankind, and in the world.

Controversy about the existence of life beyond death has concerned our ancestors inasmuch as various civilizations responded either with myths and cults from the afterlife (for instance, the ancient Egyptians or the Etruscans) or with elaborations, based on Scriptures considered sacred.

All religions satisfy a single need to build a belief system and lead people. In almost all religions there are myths: any given religion dwells in the delineation of its mythological characters. This underscores that mythology plays a significant role in religion.

Mythology is the tool religion uses to try to corroborate and attribute authenticity (= truthfulness) and pragmatism to its efforts in moral indoctrination: paraboles correspond to the "concrete" illustration of the abstract teaching religions try to offer.

Mythos is the eternal structure of religion, religion is the momentary practice of mythology. Mythology aims to establish the faiths advanced by any religion through tales and epics; religion without mythology becomes weak over time.

As for common consciousness, the soul is the vital principle of human beings and it constitutes our immaterial part, which it is the fons and origo of thought, sentiment, will, moral conscience.

The Orphic-Pythagorean tradition promoted the principle of soul survival to the body and its passage from one body to the other in renewed existences.

Democritean atomism opposed to this stance, seeing the soul as nothing more than an aggregate of atoms, destined to dissolve after death.

These two doctrines both buy into human immortality in different terms and still compete, nowadays on the matter. Religions tackle spiritual atonement in different creationist styles (immortality of the soul), while transhumanists search for artificial-scientific methods to biologically extend the life span (physical immortality).

A lot of religions have each developed forms of theology, on a revelatory basis, on a reasoning, logical or dialectical account to define the destiny and ultimate expectations of the individual (eschatology).

*In Dante's Paradiso, Dante is with Beatrice, staring at the highest heavens.*

In Christian thought, to give you an idea, eschatology is generally exemplified through the resurrection of the dead, concept of eternal life, the Day of Judgment and the Afterlife.

In the outline of many religions, it is possible to return to life after death, either as *thanatos* (passage), as *hypnos* (sleep), as *apokatástasis* (return to original state) or more extensively as *alchemy* (or longevity).

The resurrection of the flesh is the original eschatological doctrine, affirmed by both the Catholic, Orthodox and other Christian denominations, which embraces that at the end of time, after the Last Judgment, all the bodies of the dead will resurrect and rejoin their respective souls.

Christian moralism invented the problem of the *"intermediate state"* between death and the final resurrection by postulating a *conditional immortality*, whereby souls will see God only at the moment of resurrection.

For some, the resurrection of the flesh takes place in the very instant of death, but is completed only with the advent of the new world, capable of hosting a resurrected body (Boros). In Islam as in Roman Christianity, survival is a truth of faith regarding the final resurrection.

With religion, human beings are saved by faith alone (fideism). In order to help the faithful with the passage into these dimensions confidently and courageously, *"ars moriendi"* ("the art of dying well") dominated since the late Middle Ages.

Spirituality has consequently taken on the meaning of a lifestyle, originated and derived from personal religious experience, lived in the concrete of one's existence, with a long-term supernatural perspective.

By dint of numberless cultural and religious postures, spirituality is rated as a path or spiritual path, the devotee advances through to achieve a specific array of goals: a higher state of awareness (nirvana), the attainment of wisdom (from *theophania*) and communion with the divine in terms of transcendence or immanence (mysticism), which usually presupposes some form of earthly liberation from materiality (asceticism).

However, explaining the world and the universe as God's creation is a postponement of the explanation, due to the fact that the inexplicability of the universe becomes inexplicability of God.

*Theological noncognitivism*, as used in literature, ventures to refute the concept of God by showing that it is unverifiable and meaningless.

In this vein, Curry's paradox displays how the notion of First Cause - one of the most general forms the idea of God may be traced back to - turns out to be meaningless when one tries to express it, in the formal language of mathematical logic. Kant viewed the soul and its immortality as one of the postulates that practical reason must presuppose, without demonstration, for the purposes of the otherworldly agreement between virtue and happiness.

One of the revolutionary theses in defense of divine attributes and divine action is that God cannot be explained or described clearly in words, in other words, God is *ineffable*.

Moreover, the concept of causality is totally absent in the original Chinese philosophy: with the absence of an idea of God as *primum movens*, not tolerating reification means valuing practical activity and "personal growth", as superior to theological intellectualization, and spiritual conceptualization. One can be a Daoist without necessarily having a definition and explanation of what God is - a train of thought that rejects the canon whereby a path cannot be followed without a coherent, rational conceptualization.

Post-Kantians onwards, the unquestioning idea of soul dissolved, almost completely, into a more secular, utilitarian perspective: from the Aristotelian definition of form of the body and the Cartesian autonomy with respect to it into that of *subjectivistically autonomous* consciousness (Ego).

For Feuerbach, religion is the objectification of human needs and aspirations, the projection of them into an imaginary entity, which is falsely considered independent of humankind and where these aspirations are *ideally* fully realized.

With faith, believers make God in their own image and likeness through a psychic process of "absolutization of the human".

Considered one of the most important transhumanist technologies currently being developed, cryonics is the name given to the system of preserving the human body and brain, after death, in anticipation of possible future revival.

For the Greeks, death simply meant that there was no more life, therefore, the heroic end was exalted. The ancient Greeks called the quest for immortality "hubris". To "know oneself" was to know that death is inevitable. Humankind seems to believe that death is how things *should* be, that we are all *meant* to die.

In this frame of mind, transhumanism and scientific orientations concurrently trial antidotes, denying there is even an eschatological dilemma altogether and that death ought to be considered only an existential risk - a possibility, rather than a certainty, which can be treated or eliminated with technology, when addressed under a risk management framework analogous to the systemic approach we already use in all areas of life such as business, security or healthcare.

From futurologists like Huxley, Ettinger, Max More to human enhancement like gene therapy, bionics, nanostructures, eugenics has been building a post-human life, for at least two centuries, using technology as a bridge between the terrestrial and metaphysical, the mortal and the immortal, undergirded by a common belief in *auto-creationism*.

## DID YOU KNOW?

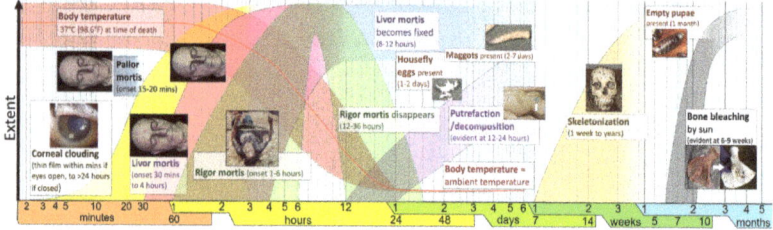

Research geared towards **extension of maximum lifespan** in humans is proceeding with development of bionic eyes, implantable artificial kidney, lab-grown hearts, artificial lungs and xenotransplantation, organ transplantation from animal species to human beings such as bioprosthetic, pig or bovine-derived artificial heart valves.

Some faiths require believers to refuse medical treatment. For example, Jehovah's Witnesses aren't allowed to receive blood transfusions, and Christian Scientists often refuse all traditional medical treatment.

Religion has a surprisingly high correlation with poverty, according to a Gallup survey conducted in more than 100 countries. The more poverty a nation has, the higher the "religiosity" in that nation. In general, richer countries are less religious than poorer ones.

# CHAPTER XII

# Politics

*The State:
Nature, Morality, Society*

---

How much control does the State have over you?

---

A State is a centralized, political organization that imposes and enforces rules over a population, within a territory. There is no unequivocal definition of a state. The legitimacy of government, in political terms "the justification for a State", ultimately depends on its ability to serve the interests of its people and secure their consent, and support.

What makes a State legitimate is a *busillis*, with a streak of philosophically-charged attempts at formulating a definitive answer.

In ancient times, many civilizations invented their own systems of government. The history of democracy can be traced back to classical Athens, where the concept of direct democracy was born, when city-states were formed.

Citizens were allowed to participate in decision-making through assemblies, courts and elected officials. The word *"democracy"* itself comes from the Greek words *demos* (people) and *kratos* (rule), designating that the powers of governing rest with the people.

In Rome, the Republic system was established to refer to the government as a "public thing" (res - publica): the supreme power lies in the people via its elected representatives. SPQR, an abbreviation for *Senatus Populusque Romans* ("the Senate and People of Rome"), is an emblematic abbreviated phrase alluding to the government of the ancient Roman Republic.

At prima facie, we may say that the power of government derives from the consent of those who are governed. Therefore, a State is legitimate only if it has the support of its citizens, who willingly follow its laws and regulations (consent of the governed).

Nineteenth-century painting by Philipp Foltz depicting the Athenian politician Pericles delivering his famous funeral oration in front of the Assembly

However, the practice of democracy gradually declined during the Middle Ages, giving way to absolute monarchies and feudal systems. Feudalism was the prevalent form of governance in Europe: people worked and fought for nobles in return for protection, and use of land.

As a result, some theorists argue that a government is legitimate simply because it has been in power for a long time and is accepted as a legitimate authority by the people (historical tradition).

The strongest version of historical tradition defends that rulers take their legitimacy from God or a higher power, therefore, their authority should not be contested or challenged (divine right theory).

Not a case, this period witnessed the rise of the Holy Roman Empire and the Church.

When Charles I inherited the thrones of England, Wales, Ireland and Scotland, he tried to rule in line with the "Divine Right of Kings": the principle that the king was directly appointed by God to rule. Like his father, King Charles I thought that a king should be able to act without having to seek approval from Parliament. When he could not get Parliament to agree with his religious and foreign policies, he tried to rule without the Parliament at all. For 11 years, he found ways to raise money without Parliament's approval but eventually trouble in Scotland meant that he had to recall Parliament.

Monarchism metamorphosed into constitutional monarchies such as United Kingdom, Spain, Monaco and Japan. Political philosophers promote monarchy as the best form of government, on the grounds that a monarch begets popular liberty and natural desire to hierarchy, non-partisanship, no private interest, long termism, civil war reduction and government accountability.

*A woodcut of the Defenestrations of Prague in 1618 —which began the Thirty Years' War and ended with the Peace of Westphalia that started the recognition of the modern state*

The Renaissance period nurtured a resurgence of ideas related to individualism, secularism and humanism. These new ideas challenged the authority of the Church and instigated the creation of nation-states toward the Age of Exploration. The Enlightenment era kicked off significant changes across the political landscape of Europe: *representative democracy* flourished with the advent of liberal political philosophy, which advocates for political freedom, equality and rationality.

Liberal thought smacks with a plausible teleology of the State. According to John Locke, the goal of the State or Commonwealth is "the preservation of property" (*Second Treatise on Government*), with "property" in Locke's work referring not only to personal possessions but also to one's life and liberty. On this account, the State is the bedrock for social cohesion and productivity, creating incentives for wealth-creation, by providing guarantees of protection for one's life, liberty and personal property.

Provision of public goods is considered by some such as Adam Smith, as a central function of the State, since these goods would otherwise be underprovided.

Sociopolitologist Charles Tilly has challenged legitimacy narratives of a State as being the result of a societal contract or provision of services in a free market – he characterized the State more akin as a protection racket in the vein of organized crime.

The concept of democracy swiftly expanded hand in hand with jurisprudence to incorporate characteristics such as freedom of assembly, freedom of religion and speech, natural justice and legal remedy, freedom from unwarranted governmental deprivation of the right to life and liberty, right of self-defence and rights of the accused.

Voting rights effectively legitimise the State by public election (suffrage) and its representatives, irrespective of inherited social class or wealth (power); the protection of property gives every person the right to peaceful enjoyment of their possessions. This imposes an obligation on the State to allow (and not to interfere with) personal ownership in its entirety, that is intangible rights such as creative work, political franchise and tangible rights like money or real estate.

*Women voter outreach (1935)*

Hence, the history of democracy equals, hereafter, a powerful story of human rights evolution and transformation.

In second thought, then, we may postulate that individuals give up some of their autonomy and submit to State authority, in exchange for protection and security. Thus, a government is legitimate only if it represents the general will of the people and serves their interests (social contract theory).

The subsequent Industrial Revolution put things in order for the development of capitalism and socialism: working-class movements and trade unions emerged to fight for workers' rights. This upgraded form of consequentialism underscored how the government is legitimate, if and only if it promotes the greatest happiness of the greatest number of people. In other words, government actions and policies should be evaluated based on their overall consequences for society (utilitarianism).

*Salus populi suprema lex esto* (Latin: "The welfare of the people shall be the supreme law") is a maxim by Cicero endorsed by Locke, Hobbes and Spinoza, since at least 1700, as a fundamental rule for government.

In the 19th and 20th centuries, democracy faced various challenges across the public and personal gradient including imperialism, fascism and communism - the last two respectively imposing a classist or classless social system.

The 20th century was swamped with two World Wars, which had a profound impact on global politics and sparked autonomy in all its declinations: independence, non-alignment but also the rise of anarchism, feminism, civil rights movement, supremacy and hegemony. USA Independence, Holocaust, Cold War, Arms race and Space Race shaped the world's political landscape, urging the development of new forms of government such as social and participatory democracy.

The pluralist approach suggested that the modern democratic State's actions are the result of pressures applied by a variety of organized interests. Political theorist Robert Dahl called this kind of State a *polyarchy*: a form of government which is neither a dictatorship nor a democracy, with power invested in multiple people.

Democracy has undergone semantic flexions, changing in meaning and significance due to these cultural, political and social charges. For example, the traditional concept of democracy has now been stretched to include minority rights, gender equality and environmental protection.

In recent years, globalization and technology have changed the way nations interact with each other. *Non-state actors* and the increasing importance of human rights has led to calls for greater accountability and transparency from governments.

A State should not be confused with a government; a government is an organization that has been granted the authority to act on the behalf of a State. Nobody sees the State and the State never acts - it is an abstract concept. This complicates the legitimacy, function and power stance of a State ten fold.

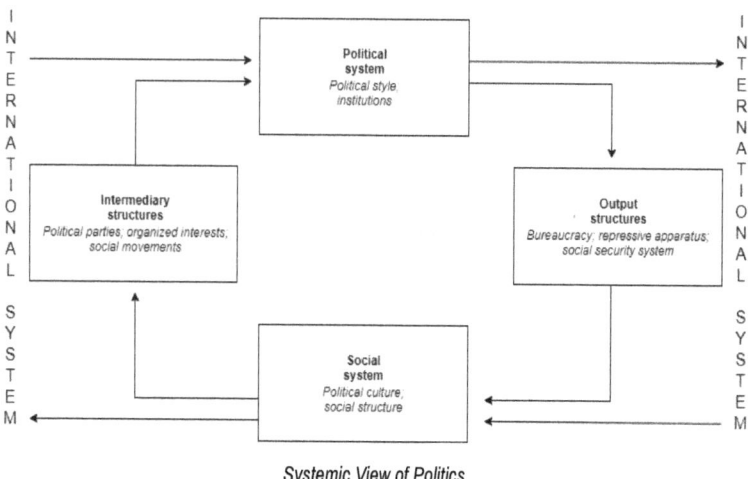

*Systemic View of Politics*

A government's power is a highly susceptible, multifaceted dance between leading a nation and complying with what the State mandates, sometimes even with "unwritten" constitution like the UK. Public service leaders, in the same way as corporate ones in private markets, have a complicated relationship with power, because their power is activated and experienced in the context of interpersonal relationships.

By virtue of their structural positions, they are simultaneously the "victims and the carriers of change" within a government, receiving strategy prescriptions from the government above and having to execute those strategies with the citizens who work beneath them.

Politics is a process of conflict; groups compete for authority and the control of scarce resources, necessarily breeding conflict between interests. Ergo, public service leaders usually find themselves stuck in between various stakeholder interests, including their own unethical temptations, which can produce "relentless and conflicting demands", despite managing self-control in decision making.

The role of government in morality and normativity is, therefore, complex and very controversial.

On one hand, the government has the responsibility to uphold and enforce the laws and regulations that are designed to protect citizens' rights and promote their well-being. This includes laws related to criminal offences, property rights, environmental protection, public health and safety.

However, governments can also play a significant role in shaping and influencing societal norms, and moral values through education, media and legislation.

In real world, governments can promote or obstruct moral values such as respect for diversity, gender equality and social justice by passing laws that prohibit or reinforce discrimination or by ensuring that educational materials reflect these values.

Utilitarians promote death penalty as retribution for victims and/or society, hence Texas and Kentucky still sentence to death those who commit murder or rape, with the electric chair as an option for execution. Law-enforcement revengeful acts of this order beg the question if capital punishment actually brings solace to the victims and most importantly, if it really punishes (or deter) crime.

Absurdly, you can be tortured and imprisoned, up to six years, in Algeria or Morocco, for same-sex sexual activity or marriage.

In China, you can be punished by lethal injection for vocal disagreement with the government (political dissidence). In Iran, those watching pornography and women dancing without a veil are sentenced to death by hanging, stoning or shooting.

In North Korea, making illegal international calls without a phone card or watching foreign medias constitutes capital crime, with execution by firing squad or decapitation.

Death penalty is a state-sanctioned practice of deliberately killing someone that subtly legitimizes a state-sanctioned immoral act (double standards) and psychological abuse with the traditional imprisonment of those convicted, and sentenced to death even for tens of years, awaiting execution (the so-called *"death row"*).

Here's how we appreciate the controversy between what Foucault hailed as the duty of surveillance and punish (*Surveiller et punir*), and the cultural history of humankind which seems to be a total different story.

When governments intervene in public, specific moral dilemmas such as euthanasia, abortion and capital punishment, they hope to balance the individual's autonomy and freedom with the common good, and social interests.

| Liberalism (Moderate) Libertarianism (Radical) Division of transactions between economic agents | |
|---|---|
| Capitalism (Moderate) Imperialism (Radical) Concentration of transactions between economic agents | Republicanism (Moderate) Equalitarianism (Radical) Specialization of transactions between economic agents |
| Corporatism (Moderate) Feudalism (Radical) Generalization of transactions between economic agents | Socialism (Moderate) Communism (Radical) Diffusion of transactions between economic agents |
| Nationalism (Moderate) Fascism (Radical) Unification of transaction between economic agents | |

*Three axis model of political ideologies with both moderate and radical versions, and the goals of their policies*

Since Magna Carta in 1215, natural justice or due process commands that the government must not be unfair to the people, by abusing them physically or mentally.

Society functions effectively and individuals' rights are protected only when a judicial system (the sovereign State) exists, however, it is essential that governments maintain a delicate balance between respecting individuals' autonomy and promoting the common good, while also being aware of the diverse cultural and ethical perspectives that exist in a pluralistic society.

Auditing the actions of the government with a referendum, a public vote on a particular issue such as a public execution or abortion law is a necessary process to review and control the legitimacy given to the State.

Any mandate should feature periodical, active scrutiny from general public, other than the indirect news media outreach or electoral campaigns which are nothing but exercises of filtering, noise dilution and obscurantism.

This safeguard measure would ensure, for instance, that the citizens unanimously ratify each and every decision taken by the Government as well as its vision, objectives and prioritisation on an annual basis, just like corporate governance already does by embedding financial audit or supervisory Boards in its execution.

Parliamentary approval may suffice, except that governing strategy is highly susceptible to representatives' beliefs (and ideological extremes), sensibility, historical and socio-intellectual background, hence a purposeful governing system is difficult to put in place.

The recent Covid-19 pandemic and more recent geopolitical events such as the war in Ukraine stress the fallacy of implying the necessity for a government with its self-sufficiency on every decision, that is, the justification for the State engenders arbitrariness (or autocratic allowance): the justification of violence and war.

To resume an earlier account, social scientist Tilly also made the case that war is an essential part of State-making; that wars create states and vice versa. Fascism, above all, regarded war as means to national rejuvenation and war bonds are still the most controversial, exorbitant debt securities issued by governments to finance military operations in times of war (e.g. Israel's $48 billion).

Most governments constitutionally inherit the right to send armed forces to war, with little or no democratic approval, usually with a highly-prejudiced reason (or "just cause"): the concept of self-defence, which validates the argument that war is never justified and exemplified worldwide by the current Russian invasion of Ukraine (2014–present) or the ongoing armed conflict between Palestinian militant groups led by Hamas and Israel.

American tanks moving in formation during the Gulf War.

No war referendum has ever taken place. The earliest idea of a war referendum came from the Marquis de Condorcet in 1793 and Immanuel Kant in 1795.

Although most states would easily renounce and repudiate warfare, citizens do not have a say when it is time to approve government's decision to go to war or raise capital to essentially kill in the name of borders; it's peremptory and in many countries, as of today, military service is also compulsory (conscription), an imposition against personal freedom in stark contrast with preferable movements such as pacifism and anti-militarism.

Another inexplicable form of the implicit consent to power relations that is gifted everyday to the State, for instance is traceable in high-capacity democracies who suffer from high levels of internal violence, prominently the United States of America.

The current, global turmoil on government accountability due to racial profiling, police brutality or specific misuse of discretion in the last decade is indicative of why the problematic justification of the State is not a question of "bad apple" individuals, or systemic abuse, rather a broader governing order grounded first in the biased politicians who provide impunity for violence.

Thus, police misconduct reveals changes must start at the political level — from campaign support by police unions to laws such as qualified immunity — rather than lying the technical burden of change with the police agencies (Rachel Klein, *A Savage Order*).

In the end, many sustain that police should be immune from prosecution, because the wrong or unfair methods used are justified if the overall goal is good (the end justifies the means) commenting the inherent, legitimate authority of the State to use or authorize their use of physical force to compel law compliance by an unwilling subject.

There is little or no independent oversight of a government, at any given time (state monopoly on violence), nor any performance measurement by its citizens who, like in Italy, for the last ten years, did not even get to vote, rather succumb to unelected, technical governments (technocracy), mostly representing an already-established elite, consequently, increasing civic apathy (failed State).

# Contemporary Political Debates

## What is the best form of government and its relationship with individuals?

One widely thought-provoking definition of a State comes from the German sociologist Max Weber who posited that a "State" is a polity - an identifiable political identity - that maintains a monopoly on the legitimate use of violence.

With the evolution of political science and democracy, disparate views blossomed on what the relationship between individuals and government should look like.

Some argue that a libertarian form of government is best to set off maximum individual freedom with limited government intervention, while others advocate for a more socialist or communist system where the government has control over resources, and may allocate them in the best interest of the society.

Magna Charta or "Charter" *was one of the world's first documents containing commitments by a sovereign to his people to respect certain legal rights.*

With hindsight, the ideal relationship between people and government would be one where the State ensures the protection of individuals' rights, provides public services and infrastructure, perpetuates law and order, and promotes equal opportunities for all citizens (utopia).

The concept of citizenship has evolved over time in history as opposed to anarchism, a political philosophy that vows for a society in statelessness condition - a "voluntary institution of self-government".

Citizenship refers to the rights, privileges and duties that individuals have as members of a nation or State. This includes access to basic human rights such as education, healthcare and social security, as well as political and legal rights such as the right to vote, and the right to a fair trial.

In ancient Greece, citizenship was limited to a select few who were born into privileged families (oligarchy). They had the right to participate in the city-state's political and economic activities, while others, including slaves and women, were excluded.

In the ternary theory of forms of government (of one, of a few, of many, i.e. respectively monarchy, oligarchy, democracy), aristocracy represents the non-deviated form of oligarchy.

In its original and most proper meaning, aristocracy is the prevalence, the government of the most deserving, understood as those who are morally and intellectually the best or the most valiant, historically identified with the patricians - those who, by right of blood (*Jus sanguinis*) belong to the highest class of society, the nobles who hold power.

During the Enlightenment, the concept of citizenship mushroomed to include all individuals as equal members of society, regardless of their social status or birthright. This idea was buttressed by the French Revolution, declaring human and citizen rights as universal (*Declaration of the Rights of Man and of the Citizen*, 1789).

In anarchism, the notion of citizenship has been viewed critically. Anarchists reject the use of a centralized authority and believe in a society where individuals have the freedom to govern themselves, without the need for laws and regulations imposed by the State.

Anarchists believe in a direct democracy where every individual has an equal say in decision-making, and where power is decentralized. They oppose the concept of nationality and consider themselves belonging to a global community of individuals who fight against oppression, and exploitation.

"No War but the Class War"
Black bloc protesters parading anarcho-communism imagery

Libertarians stand up for the rights of minorities and marginalized groups, including refugees, immigrants and indigenous communities. They envision a world where everyone is treated equally and has access to the same resources, and opportunities, regardless of their citizenship status.

Overall, the theory of citizenship has opened out across the ages and with the advent of anarchism. While citizenship, in a traditional connotation, may bring certain benefits and protections, anarchists challenge the value of a centralized state and push for a society where individuals have more direct control over their lives, and communities.

As a result, the "best" form of government is subjective and depends on various factors, like cultural values, historical background, economic situation and societal goals.

Different forms of government such as democracy, monarchy, communism, socialism, authoritarianism and others, have their advantages and disadvantages.

The terms *"right wing"* and *"left wing"* originated in the French Revolution of 1789, with the right wing representing aristocratic and conservative interests, and the left wing representing the interests of the common people and progressives.

In Europe, the right wing has historically been associated with conservative and nationalist parties, while the left wing has been associated with socialist and social democratic parties. In the United States, the political spectrum is often divided into Republicans on the right and Democrats on the left, although the meanings of those terms have evolved over time, flexing regionally and ideologically.

Over the centuries, both right and left wing political movements have had varying degrees of influence and success, depending on the social and economic conditions of their countries. Right wing movements included Fascism in Italy and Nazism in Germany, while historical left wing included communism in the Soviet Union and social democracy in Scandinavian countries.

Today, the terms right wing and left wing have come to signify a wide range of political positions and ideologies, and are often brandished to describe political parties, currents, and individuals who hold a certain set of beliefs and values, with moderation.

The left wing has been terribly busy, across the history, fomenting the masses against class oppression and the fear thereof, in comparison with the better-off peasants ("kulaks").

Yet, even diehard fans of economic equality against the so-called "enemies of the people" have realised that doing socialism is a hoax, especially after capitulating to the revived communism of social media, the news media show trials, agitprop and tyrannical culture industry.

Today, communists still pursue policies of social indoctrination through left-wing propaganda in education and the media.

Wth a "woke" narrative, they persuade the "weak" to transmute any personal problem in social business, exploit the defence mechanism of the minorities with low self-esteem who want to feel accepted, and leverage their resentment to make believe society is a mere individualistic play-field - without a presumed following of the interests of a compromised structure (an individualist need not be an egoist).

The leftist articles of faith get across that everyone can have everything, without any difference or effort, everyone is equal, everyone can have a say, only by virtue of the fact that we exist. Bear in mind, most of us fundamentally share all their causes but inclusion is not illusion.

Conservative version of the left-wing progressive outburst, fascism presented itself as an opportunistic alternative to both international socialism and free-market capitalism. Like collectivists, fascists have commonly sought to eliminate the autonomy of large-scale capitalism and relegate it to the state.

In that sense, as established by the philosopher creator of fascist ideology, Giovanni Gentile, fascism is a form of socialism, a type of authoritarian ultra-nationalist communism.

Converging in the determination to achieving results by suppressing opposition, the ideologies of *communism* and *fascism* together brought an orgy of violence, killed billions and led humanity to despair, with reminiscence still surrounding us.

Either is a political scam, because the ugly truth, and the "beauty" is that

> "All animals are equal, but some animals are more equal than others."

A proclamation by the pigs who control the government in the novel *Animal Farm* by George Orwell, the sentence is a comment on the hypocrisy of governments that proclaim the absolute equality of their citizens, yet give power and privileges to a small elite.

Nobody, in principle, is against equality, national pride, self sufficiency but we are all born unequal, and what may seem ingenious in the ideological state (socialism) that aspires to communism (post-scarcity world), has proven to be impractical (dictatorship or like with Nazism, tyranny).

In the last 140 years there have been 106 major famines, each resulting in more than 100,000 deaths. The death rate was particularly high in socialist countries such as the Soviet Union, China, Cambodia, Ethiopia and North Korea, where tens of millions of people died due to the forced transfer of means of production from private to public, and the use of hunger as a weapon such as Holodomor.

Now it's not grand aristocratic families, Mussolini or Russian Marxist revolutionaries, it's Silicon Valley Big Tech companies but as new as these dynamics may seem, we succumb to an identical system of ownership: the most class-conscious are tricked into parting with their property (money, identity, confidential information etc.) to secure a greater enjoyment of human rights, or social power, only to discover later that it was bait to get your data, and an "ultra democratic" communist state will never realize.

And if anybody above you doesn't like something, or you don't follow what they tell you, you are ousted, dispossessed and socially confined in the phygital oblivion (Shadowbanning, cancel culture), on par with what Bandenbekämpfung or anti-partisan operations used to do.

Restoration of the property is, of course, strenuous in a case of technocrats holding property wrongly because it deprives the holder of the use of the property, while the case is awaiting trial, up and including the rights of the defence and reply, thereby putting pressure on the holder to leave the property behind.

Young people have heard much about the "evils of capitalism" against right-wing parties, but too little about the "evils of socialism", which they unwittingly subscribe to, nowadays, by upholding left-wing propaganda - investment thesis of countless foundations, university endowment funds, charities, and digital business models.

Socialist and leftist political organizations are still engaged in anti-capitalism and resist Realpolitik, with a subliminal memo to chill, riot and stay lazy, in a cuckoo land where anyone owns everything, what-if labour gets the same results for everybody in equal parts, and there is no need to distinguish oneself from others or outperform the elite through hard-earned merit, as opposed to inherited or lucked one like the majority of the radical chic.

In 1987, Harry Frankfurt brilliantly taught that

> "In itself, economic equality has no particular moral relevance. Looking at the distribution of economic goods, what is important from a moral point of view is not that everyone has the same goods, but that each of us has enough."

Marx envisioned a society where workers owned the means of production. In real-world communism Marxism fails, because governments despotically own the means of production.

In the grip of communist nostalgia, democrats still violently ram together rife contradictions within society: the obsession with social identification and validity, the urge to disappear into collective possession and eventually, the abolition of the private or total dissolution of the much fought-for individuality.

> "Disparity in income and wealth is a fundamental characteristic of the market economy. Its elimination would entirely destroy this type of economy. [...] The most despotic system of government that history has ever known, Bolshevism, presents itself as the true embodiment of the principle of equality and freedom of all men. But the liberal champions of equality before the law knew very well that men are born unequal and that it is precisely their inequality that generates social cooperation and civilization."
>
> **LUDWIG VON MISES, *HUMAN ACTION: A TREATISE ON ECONOMICS, 1949***

To the chagrin of socialism, therefore, capitalism has made us all richer in the world. China itself ironically demonstrates that capitalism is a good economic system for reducing poverty compared to others.

The "Chinese miracle" occurred because, after Mao's death, free market reforms were initiated and private property rights were introduced. Year after year, statistics show that no one dies of hunger or dreams in the countries with the greatest economic freedom.

In stark contrast, economic repression leads to hunger and poverty, as we have seen again in Venezuela, where 10% of the population has already emigrated to escape hunger under the country's socialist regime.

It is only on the strength of industrialization, technological progress and the free market that we have managed to guarantee such a high level of well-being to the majority of the world's population, in an extremely short period of time.

Ultimately, it is up to the citizens of each country to decide which form of government best suits their needs and aspirations.

But taking the points made so far seriatim, it is beyond the shadow of a doubt that "socialism is for the rich and capitalism is for the poor". Communism ruthlessly is a route to plutocracy - rule by the wealthy - and the only successful citizen being one who has rights, by virtue of wealth. Wealth is to be created by enterprises, though and their autonomous labour; what lies with the State is only to imagine "good" rules.

In this sense, the anti-capitalist complaint that more resources flow to the rich than to the poor is a loose interpretation, without depth.

The rich create jobs and government income, with companies, investments, not the poor and it is only fair that those who have, give [and are fiscally motivated] to enrich society, unexpectedly also favouring those averse to a rags-to-riches life, such as free-riders.

At the same time, economic freedom creates equal opportunities for all classes, if any, beyond systemic vices such as racism, transphobia or sexism which, although to be extinguished as soon as possible, are no longer public characteristics in the welfare state, rather popular fads.

All these are rooted in classism, currently discontinued off the back of capitalism, yet enjoying lifeblood after the fall of socialist regimes, just because leftists are still so avariciously melodramatic about it.

Of course, the road to permanently eradicating poverty or inequality is still tortuous. But the path is clear: turning our backs on the free market would make us all poorer.

Resolution of these problems comes slow because, just like in the corporate world, strategy without execution is nothing. And the difficulty in making changes is also exacerbated because governments, by nature, have branches.

Separation of powers is a political concept that refers to the division of government responsibilities, and powers among different divisions of government. The trichotomy is based on the idea that concentrating too much power in any one branch of government can lead to tyranny, corruption and abuse of power. The three main branches of government are usually identified as the executive, legislative and judicial branches.

The executive branch is responsible for enforcing laws and policies; it is typically headed by a president or a Prime Minister.

The legislative branch is responsible for making laws; it is typically made up of a parliament, congress or other governing body. The judicial branch is responsible for interpreting laws and ensuring that they are applied fairly and consistently; it is typically made up of courts and judges.

Different forms of government can also affect the distribution of power among these branches. A presidential system such as the United States, separates the executive and legislative branches more clearly than a parliamentary system such as the United Kingdom, where the executive branch is made up of members of the legislative branch.

A monarchy such as Saudi Arabia, may have a less clear separation of powers due to the concentration of power in the monarchy.

One of the founders of modern political philosophy, Thomas Hobbes addressed the conflict of the legitimacy and form of the State, with an influential formulation of social contract theory in his book *Leviathan* (1651). The State is thereby represented as a giant made up of many distinct individuals; the giant holds a sword in one hand, symbol of temporal power, and in the other the crozier, symbol of religious power. According to Hobbes, the two powers should not be separated.

Nonetheless, the separation of powers is a key element in many forms of State: the division helps to ensure that no single branch of government has too much control as well as that laws, policies are created and enforced fairly, and effectively.

Since politics involves the use of power and authority to govern, political activity has become coveted and manipulative, filled with many euphemistic, metaphorical expressions to win over citizens and in order for social climbers to join the institutional hierarchy, thus commonly perceived as an attempt to "obscure, mislead and confuse" for mere selfish purposes.

Politicians are known for their rhetoric, the art of using language effectively to persuade or influence others. They use different oratorical techniques such as emotional appeals, logical arguments and persuasive language to gain support from the public. They also use rhetoric to frame issues in a way that favours their position and to discredit opposing viewpoints. However, the excessive use of rhetoric (eristic) can lead to propaganda, misinformation and manipulation, thus eroding democracy's core values.

It is essential to communicate, govern and make politics responsibly in order to promote a healthy discourse of ideas as much as democratic accountability, and transparency.

And the pernicious lack thereof is why actual progress is pausing, every now and then.

Take the healthcare system, which in many countries has come under scrutiny, with proponents of universal coverage arguing that every citizen should have access to affordable healthcare, while opponents argue that such a system would be too costly and ineffective.

Unresolved points include the cryptic role of private insurance companies, the cost of prescription drugs and the efficiency of a healthcare delivery system.

Immigration has taken to be another contentious issue in many countries, with some arguing for stricter border control and restrictions on illegal migration, while others stand up for a more open and inclusive approach like the Schengen Area, the open border area with no passport control policy of the European Union.

The debate often revolves around matters of national security, economic impact and human rights.

The wealth gap between the rich and poor is a growing issue in many societies, with troubles over the causes of income inequality, and the best strategies to address it. Solutions range from increasing the minimum wage, progressive taxation to investing in education and training programs.

Globalization has driven the world to unprecedented levels of international trade, but some argue that free trade agreements have also created job losses and inequality, particularly in developed economies. Pundits maintain that trade is essential for economic growth and national development, that is, trade barriers hurt consumers and businesses alike.

The United States trade embargo against Cuba is the most enduring economic sanction in modern history and prevents U.S. businesses from conducting trade with Cuban interests; it cost the Cuban economy $1.1 trillion in the 55 years since its inception.

Issues related to social justice such as race, gender and LGBTQ+ rights, continue to be at the forefront of political debates.

While many have made strides towards equality, others believe that there is still work to be done to ensure that everyone suffering from minority stress, segregation, discrimination, harassment, bashing or hate crime is treated fairly and with more inclusion (e.g. disability, intersex, same-sex parenting, gender apartheid).

Unisex public toilets

There is a wrangle over the extent of climate change and the best strategies to address it. Some argue that climate change is a natural occurrence and that human activity has little impact on it, while opponents counter argue that humans are the primary cause of climate change and that we must take immediate action to reduce carbon emissions, by shifting to renewable energy sources.

Education is another major hot topic in many countries, with war of words over funding, standardized testing and the role of government in education. Many advocate for more student-centered and innovative approaches to learning, while the opposition recommends traditional methods and standardized curriculum.

The role of the government in foreign affairs is a controversial subject as well, with perplexity on military intervention, diplomacy and alliances. One half vindicates that the government should prioritize national interests and security, whereas the other half campaigns for a more multilateral approach that values cooperation and peacekeeping.

Clash over digital privacy and data security is serious, as technology advances. Debates center around government surveillance, corporate data collection and consumer rights.

The nothing to hide argument admonishes that individuals have no reason to fear or oppose surveillance programs like Carnivore, access to the bulk communications citizens provide at different locations or espionage, unless they are afraid it will uncover their own illicit activities.

Cryptography such as Tor, VPNs and Deep Web is mainly used for protecting user privacy, secure transactions and avoid a central issuing or regulating authority. On the horizon, this attitude aligns a lot with anti-dictatorship efforts and anarchism, while being an increasingly popular tool for organised crime groups to conduct illicit activities and money laundering.

Some make a case for greater privacy protections, while others favour increased surveillance and data sharing to combat cyber threats.

The dispute over gun control revolves, instead, around balancing the fallacy perpetuating "individual-right" to keep and bear arms (as found in the Second Amendment to the U.S. Constitution), with public safety concerns. Some contend that gun ownership is a fundamental right that should not be restricted, while others defend that stricter gun control measures are necessary to reduce gun violence.

Guns are deeply ingrained in American society with more mass shootings and the highest civilian gun ownership than any other country: open carry, gun shows loophole and unfettered, misconstrued gun rights or sanctuary, driven by the all-American grassroots culture that values all things brash, self-made, arrogant and insensitive.

Exponents of economic reform also defend that healthcare should be free for everyone, that all people should receive a basic income and rich people should pay more taxes.

Promoters of equality and social reform, for instance, affirm that drug addicts should get help not punishment, prisoners should be able to vote, men and women should be allowed to compete against each other in the Olympics, and governments shouldn't track their citizens.

Every principal institution of State should be clearly divided, with a blueprint for the defense of its autonomy and independence, compared to the other powers of the state governments.

Broadly speaking, the Constitution recognizes every single official, including the judges, to be directly liable for the damages caused in the exercise of their duties. Today, however, judges unlike all other government officials, cannot be held accountable directly.

Jurisdictions ensure accountability to more senior judges through the judicial system, by enabling appeal to a higher court and subordination to a Lord Chief Justice through the complaints route.

The point is, however, that none of these actions actually hold judges accountable for their behaviour. At worst, a judge would recuse themselves or be *"recused"* from the case, that is, simply be removed from the judicial decision-making with a replacement or a "decree of nullity" obtained by means of appeal: a review of the trial by a higher level judge.

A common appeal is that a decision from the judge was incorrect such as whether to suppress certain evidence or to impose a certain sentence.

Errors for judicial bias rising from impartiality and conflicts of interests are the biggest issue: politics has seen its voice progressively grow within the judiciary, particularly leaning toward the red-washing and left-wing political orientation.

A recent example that shows a bad case of political bias in judicial system includes the 45th President of the United States and Republican Leader Donald Trump being indicted by Alvin Bragg, a Democratic Manhattan District Attorney in a supposedly neutral trial stretched to fit a political agenda, despite the case having probable cause. The most striking European equivalent was certainly former Italian Prime Minister Berlusconi, whose rolling criminal trials in the last ten years, albeit reasonable, came to constitute a manifest judicial persecution orchestrated by magistrates close to left-wing parties and ideologies (the unionised *Democratic Magistracy*), who would leverage justice for the purposes of political party supremacy.

Right to the chase, away from political doors, prosecutors should face repercussions (suspension, termination, disbarment) when their indictments are dismissed as flawed for reasons that result from their faux pas or misconduct, such as presenting a case when they knew the statute of limitations was expired, or their key witness was a proven liar or when motivated by conscious, subjective bias such as lobbying.

Without the risk of repercussions there is nothing to prevent prosecutorial misconduct or malicious prosecution done for political or any partisan reason.

From the cabinet to the State functions, we reach a genuine, summative reflection on how the absence of any form of performance measurement making "scrutiny on slack" real within public sector entities, as opposed to any public or private organisations, is the jet-fuel of top-down incompetent, lazy, overprotected and entitled public servants.

## DID YOU KNOW? ▼

During the Scottish Enlightenment, John Law distinguished money as a means of exchange, from national wealth dependent on trade. Adam Smith proposed the famous idea of the *"invisible hand"* and created the concept of GDP (Gross Domestics Product).

Economics was originally politics or "political economy" and the concept of developing countries is a hoax. The entire African continent is supposed to be prosperous but it is the testing ground for weapons manufactured by developed countries, where toxic waste is dumped and it is also the ground that once harbored diamonds and oil which are now safely kept and utilised in developed countries.

Between 1928 and 2013, a broad index of US stocks increased 2,000-fold; however, 20 times they actually lost at least 20% of their value in that period. Volatility wouldn't create as much fear, if everyone realized how common it is.

# References and Bibliography

*Gettier problem*. (2023, September 26). Wikipedia. https://en.wikipedia.org/wiki/Gettier_problem

*Existence of God*. (2004, April 27). Wikipedia. https://en.wikipedia.org/wiki/Existence_of_God

*Problem of evil*. (2023, November 6). Wikipedia. https://en.wikipedia.org/wiki/Problem_of_evil

*Definitions of knowledge*. (2023, September 28). Wikipedia. https://en.wikipedia.org/wiki/Definitions_of_knowledge#Justified_true_belief

*Epistemology*. (2023, November 9). Wikipedia. https://en.wikipedia.org/wiki/Epistemology

*Problem of the criterion*. Kevin McCain, Internet Encyclopedia of Philosophy. https://iep.utm.edu/problem-of-the criterion/#:~:text=The%20Problem%20of%20the%20Criterion%20is%20the%20ancient%20problem%20of,Academic%20Skeptics%20and%20the%20Stoics.

*Unknowability*. (2023, July 8). Wikipedia. https://en.wikipedia.org/wiki/Unknowability

*Contextualism*. (2023, June 3). Wikipedia. https://en.wikipedia.org/wiki?curid=1029178

*Problem of evil*. (2023, November 6). Wikipedia. https://en.wikipedia.org/wiki?curid=30104

*Universal value*. (2023, April 23). Wikipedia. https://en.wikipedia.org/wiki?curid=3445285

*Time.* (2023, October 21). *Wikipedia.* https://en.wikipedia.org/wiki/Time

*User:FrankP/Time.* (n.d.). *Wikipedia.* https://en.wikipedia.org/wiki/User:FrankP/Time

*Normative ethics.* (2023, September 12). *Wikipedia.* https://en.wikipedia.org/wiki/Normative_ethics

*Belief.* (2023, November 9). *Wikipedia.* https://en.wikipedia.org/wiki?curid=102883

*Christian theology.* (2021, October 28). *Wikipedia.* https://en.wikipedia.org/wiki?curid=27968837

*Logic.* (2023, November 9). *Wikipedia.* https://en.wikipedia.org/wiki/Logic

*Knowledge.* (2023, November 8). *Wikipedia.* https://en.wikipedia.org/wiki/Knowledge

*Religious responses to the problem of evil.* (2023o, October 8). *Wikipedia.* https://en.wikipedia.org/wiki?curid=66827071

*Formal logic.* (2023, November 9). *Wikipedia.* https://en.wikipedia.org/wiki/Logic#Formal_logic

*Non-cognitivism.* (2023, June 26). *Wikipedia.* https://en.wikipedia.org/wiki/Non-cognitivism

*State (polity).* (2023, October 26). *WikiMili.com.* https://wikimili.com/en/State_%28polity%29

*Ruse de guerre.* (2023, June 17). *WikiMili.com.* https://wikimili.com/en/Ruse_de_guerre

*Correlates of crime.* (2023, August 20). *WikiMili.com.* https://wikimili.com/en/Correlates_of_crime

*Public Religion Research Institute.* (2023, September 22). *WikiMili.com.* https://wikimili.com/en/Public_Religion_Research_Institute

*Criticism of religion.* (2023, November 6). *WikiMili.com.* https://wikimili.com/en/Criticism_of_religion

*Linda Elder.* (2023, January 17). *WikiMili.com.* https://wikimili.com/en/Linda_Elder

*History of terrorism.* (2023, November 8). WikiMili.com. https://wikimili.com/en/History_of_terrorism

*War referendum.* (2023, November 7). WikiMili.com. https://wikimili.com/en/War_referendum

*Milestones in legal Culture and Tradition.* (2023, March 22). Berkeley Law. https://www.law.berkeley.edu/research/the-robbins-collection/exhibitions/milestones-legal-culture-tradition/

*The Roman-Dutch legal tradition.* (2023, May 5). Berkeley Law. https://www.law.berkeley.edu/research/the-robbins-collection/exhibitions/roman-dutch-legal-tradition-2/

*The Medieval Law School.* (2023, May 18). Berkeley Law. https://www.law.berkeley.edu/research/the-robbins-collection/exhibitions/medieval-law-school/

(2019, March 25). *Difference between sound and unsound argument.* DifferenceBetween.com. https://www.differencebetween.com/difference-between-sound-and-unsound-argument/

UN Watch. (2017, March 31). *UN Watch director's challenge to Arab regimes: "Where Are Your Jews?"* Canada Free Press. https://canadafreepress.com/article/un-watch-directors-challenge-to-arab-regimes-where-are-your-jews

Banerji, R. (2021, February 5). Tricky Logical Reasoning Questions with Answers. *IndiaTimes*. https://www.indiatimes.com/lifestyle/self/12-logical-reasoning-questions-thatll-have-you-stumped-in-no-time-233714.html

*Historiography.* (n.d.). Britannica Kids. https://kids.britannica.com/scholars/article/William-Jennings-Bryan/108622

(n.d.). *Frege's problem: Referential opacity.* Internet Encyclopedia of Philosophy. https://iep.utm.edu/page/3/?cat=-1

Zitelmann, R. (2020, July 27). Anyone Who Doesn't Know The Following Facts About Capitalism Should Learn Them. *Forbes*. https://www.forbes.com/sites/rainerzitelmann/2020/07/27/anyone-who-doesnt-know-the-following-facts-about-capitalism-should-learn-them/?sh=66af1fca3dc1

Zambrano, H. (n.d.). Ben-Shahar_Tal_-_The_Pursuit_of_Perfect.pdf - PDF free download. *tips*. https://idoc.tips/ben-shahartal-thepursuitofperfectpdf-pdf-free.html

UN Watch. (2017, March 30). *Video goes viral: 2.5 million worldwide view UN Watch director's challenge to Arab regimes: "Where Are Your Jews?"* UN Watch. https://unwatch.org/video-goes-viral-2-5-million-worldwide-view-un-watch-directors-challenge-arab-regimes-jews/

Lloyd, M. (2016, July 25). *Masha Lloyd's blog.* http://mashalloyd.blogspot.com/2016/07/eladios-mother-came-to-stay.html

Goodbread, J. (2023, March 14). *24 Investing statistics You must know.* Financially Simple. https://financiallysimple.com/24-interesting-investing-statistics-you-must-know/

Mitchell, H. (2017, November 10). 16 batshit historical fashion facts that'll blow your damn mind. *BuzzFeed.* https://www.buzzfeed.com/hilarywardle/giant-dresses-and-lotus-scented-lard

Mbabazize, P. M. (2014). *Rurality and rural poverty: what it means to be poor new realities, new choices for tomorrow* (PhD Thesis, Nkumba University). https://www.journalijar.com/uploads/35_THESIS-0786.pdf

*Death* (n.d.). Wikizero. https://www.wikizero.com/m/Death

*Logic* (n.d.). Wikizero. https://wikizero.com/www/Logic

Remhof, J. (2018, February 13). *"God is dead": Nietzsche and the Death of God.* 1000-Word Philosophy: An Introductory Anthology. https://1000wordphilosophy.com/2018/02/13/nietzsche-and-the-death-of-god/

Doyle, L. (2020, July 15). *What is the most interesting fact ever?* ICI 2016. https://ici2016.org/what-is-the-most-interesting-fact-ever/

Fröhlich, S. (2019, August 22). *Africa: East Africa's forgotten slave trade.* allAfrica. https://allafrica.com/stories/201908230055.html

Bath & Unwind Beauty Blog. (n.d.). *Tips & tricks.* https://blog.bathandunwind.com/category/tips-tricks/

Shuttleworth, M. (2016, April 27). *Falsifiability – Karl Popper's basic scientific principle.* Brewminate: A Bold Blend of News and Ideas. https://brewminate.com/falsifiability-karl-poppers-basic-scientific-principle/

Dane, L. (2006). *Giving chase.* Samhain Publishing. https://dokumen.pub/giving-chase-1599982595-9781599982595.html

Wikipedia contributors. (2023, September 30). *Replevin.* Wikipedia. https://en.wikipedia.org/wiki?curid=1215840

(2018, February 14). *Odd laws and traditions.* https://present5.com/odd-laws-and-traditions-it-is-illegal/

Gregory, E. (2023, May 26). *Interesting and fun facts about classical music.* Spinditty. https://spinditty.com/genres/interesting-fun-facts-about-classical-music

Tiaz, J. (2023, August 24). *25 Linguistics facts No one knows.* Tech25. https://tech25s.com/25-linguistics-facts-no-one-knows/

De Mol, L. (2018). Turing machines. In Edward N. Zalta (ed.), *Stanford Encyclopedia of Philosophy.* https://leibniz.stanford.edu/previews/sample/turing-machine-sample.pdf

Cohen, J. (2017, November 10). *Transhumanism: Can technology defeat Death?* https://www.talkdeath.com/transhumanism-can-technology-defeat-death/

*11 Facts about World Religions.* (n.d.). DoSomething.org. https://www.dosomething.org/us/facts/11-facts-about-world-religions

*Muhammad (Maometto).* (2013). Englishgratis. https://www.englishgratis.com/elingue/elingue/en/wikimag/serie11/19.htm

Kulube, L. (2019, November 1). *The slave trade in East Africa.* Chocolate Boy Ltd. https://www.chocolateboyltd.co.uk/blogs/news/the-slave-trade-in-east-africa?page=1

Doyle, L. (2020, April 18). *What does appealing a sentence mean?* ICI 2016. https://ici2016.org/what-does-appealing-a-sentence-mean/

Pant, B. (2022). Euthanasia: Are we ready for it, or is it too late? *Nepal Journal of Neuroscience, 19*(4), 1–2. https://doi.org/10.3126/njn.v19i4.51589

Know it Buddy. (2016, February 18). *Apple think different.* https://knowitbuddy.blogspot.com/2016/02/

https://speedypaper.x10.mx/argumentative-essay-topics-with-statistics.html

Wikipedia contributors. (2023, November 2). *Human rights.* Wikipedia. https://en.wikipedia.org/wiki/Human_rights

Vidani, P. (n.d.). *Creeping Sharia.* Tumblr. https://creepingsharia.tumblr.com/

Payne, S. G. (1980). *Fascism: Comparison and definition.* University of Wisconsin Press.

Summit Daily. (n.d.). *Commentary*. https://www.summitdaily.com/opinion/guest-commentary/

Schroeder-Heister, P. (2001). Popper, Karl Raimund (1902–94). In *Elsevier eBooks* (pp. 11727–11733). https://doi.org/10.1016/b0-08-043076-7/00322-3

The Economist. (2021, September 23). *Religious belief really does seem to draw the sting of poverty*. https://www.economist.com/science-and-technology/religious-belief-really-does-seem-to-draw-the-sting-of-poverty/21804961

Warter, I., & Warter, L. (2018). A cross-cultural perspective on autopsy. *Romanian Journal of Legal Medicine, 26*(1), 76-81.

N. (n.d.). *KBC questions*. https://ngururaj.blogspot.com/2009/03/

The Investopedia Team. (2023, March 22). *Marxism: What it is and comparison to communism, socialism, and capitalism*. Investopedia. https://www.investopedia.com/terms/m/marxism.asp

(2014). *there is this one man who killed his mother, was born before his father and married over 100 women without - Science*. Meritnation.com. https://www.meritnation.com/ask-answer/question/there-is-this-one-man-who-killed-his-mother-was-born/science/8012045

Baronett, S. (2008). *Logic*. Pearson Education India.

Audretsch, D. B., & Lehmann, E. E. (2023). Narrative entrepreneurship: bringing (his) story back to entrepreneurship: Narrative entrepreneurship: bringing (his) story back to entrepreneurship. *Small Business Economics, 60*(4), 1593-1612.

Freer, S. (2015). *Modernist mythopoeia: The Twilight of the gods*. Springer.

(n.d.). *The old Navy Sailor*. https://theoldnavysailor.blogspot.com/2012/07/

Olsen, T. (2002, April 1). 1986 Abortion protest case goes to Supreme Court for second time. *com*. https://www.christianitytoday.com/ct/2002/aprilweb-only/4-22-21.0.html

Kittichaisaree, K. (2020). *International Human Rights Law and Diplomacy*. Edward Elgar Publishing.

(n.d.). *Amazing medical facts of the body*. https://www.medindia.net/facts/

Misiroglu, G. (n.d.). *The handy answer book for kids (and parents), second edition.* VDOC.PUB. https://vdoc.pub/documents/the-handy-answer-book-for-kids-and-parents-second-edition-7l13fr4ikkt0

Wikipedia contributors. (2023h, October 22). *2015 European migrant crisis.* Wikipedia. https://en.m.wikipedia.org/wiki/2015_European_migrant_crisis

com. (n.d.). *FiloSofieOnline.com./ domain for sale.* https://www.hugedomains.com/domain_profile.cfm?d=filosofieonline.com

(n.d.). *Change Your Gun Laws Research Paper.* https://www.bartleby.com/essay/Change-Your-Gun-Laws-Research-Paper-PJLCYMQYWZB

Gopalan, R. (2016, February 10). *Is this grammatically correct? – Probably not!.* WP Reviews, Resources, Tips & Tricks. https://wpr2t2.com/is-this-grammatically-correct/

Shaffer, B. (2017, October 25). *5 interesting facts of music history.* Paly Your Part. https://www.playyourpartmusic.com/5-interesting-facts-of-music-history/

American Compliance Portal. (n.d.). *Argumentative essay about gun control.* http://complianceportal.american.edu/argumentative-essay-about-gun-control.php

(2011). *Einstein's relativity made easy.* http://cuckoostuff.blogspot.com/2011/09/

Wikipedia contributors. (2023j, November 7). *Politics.* Wikipedia. https://en.wikipedia.org/wiki/Politics

Smart, J. C. (Ed.). (2008). *Higher education: Handbook of theory and research* (Vol. 23). Springer Science & Business Media.

Pant, B. (2022). Euthanasia: Are we ready for it, or is it too late?. *Nepal Journal of Neuroscience, 19*(4), 1-2

*Open Life in the UK: a guide for new residents.* (2013). law.resource.org. https://law.resource.org/pub/uk/life/uk.tso.life.2013/uk.tso.life.2013.html

Fulcher, J., & Scott, J. (2011). *Sociology.* Oxford University Press, USA.

(n.d.). *Trade Quotes (181 quotes).* https://www.goodreads.com/quotes/tag/trade

Ebrahim, Y. (2020). *Regional bioclimatic architecture 1.0: in the beginning and introduction.* Ebenergy Enterprises.

Schweitzer, F., & Perry, M. (2005). *Anti-Semitism: Myth and hate from antiquity to the present.* Springer

University of London International Programmes Publications Office (2013 - 2022), *Undergraduate study in Philosophy - Academic Programme and Subject Guides.* University of London

*The Narcissistic-Masochist Character. (1988) Arnold M. Cooper. The Analytic Press.*

*Theories of Meaning.* Stanford Encyclopedia of Philosophy

*Tarski's Theory of Truth,* Massachusetts Institute of Technology, http://web.mit.edu/24.242/www/Tarskitruth.pdf

*Giannetti Anna, Architect and Engineer, Op. cit., 47, Edizioni Il Centro, Naples, Jan 1980 https://opcit.it/cms/?p=106*

*https://en.wikipedia.org/wiki/Engineering*

*Bjerklie, David. "The Art of Renaissance Engineering."Jan./Feb.1998: 54–59*

Giovanni Fanelli, Brunelleschi, Becocci, *Florence (1980),* Chapter: The Dome pp. 10–41

Fotheringham, A. S.; Rogerson, P. A (2008). *The Modifiable Areal Unit Problem* (MAUP). Sage. pp. 105–124. ISBN 978-1-4129-1082-8.

*https://en.wikipedia.org/wiki/Scale_(geography)*

Rebecca Sohn, Doris Elin Urrut. *Astronomical Unit: How far away is the sun?* https://www.space.com/17081-how-far-is-earth-from-the-sun.html

Christos A. Tsekos, Thaleia Petsiou *Environment and Philosophy: The Aesthetics and the Natural Environment,* Department of Environmental and Natural Resources Management, University of Patras, Patras, Greece and Department of Agricultural Technology, Technological Educational Institute of Epirus, City, Greece, 2018

# Recommended Reading List

- *On the Shortness of Life*, Seneca the Younger
- *The Consolation of Philosophy*, Boethius
- *The Praise of Folly*, Desiderius Erasmus of Rotterdam
- *The Myth of Sisyphus*, Albert Camus
- *The Art of Being Right: 38 Ways to Win an Argument*, Arthur Schopenhauer
- *The Art of Insulting*, Arthur Schopenhauer
- *The World as Will and Representation*, Arthur Schopenhauer
- *On the Genealogy of Morality: A Polemic*, Friedrich Nietzsche
- *The Antichrist*, Friedrich Nietzsche
- *Creative Evolution*, Henri Bergson
- *The God Delusion*, Richard Dawkins
- *Gender Trouble*, Judith Butler
- *Pedagogy of the Oppressed*, Paulo Freire
- *Ten Philosophical Mistakes*, Mortimer J. Adler
- *What We Owe to Each Other*, T. M. Scanlon

**Vincent Bozzino** (1996) became known as a poet, in Europe, when he was 14 years old, with his first collection *"On My Comet's Tail"*, commended at the Turin International Book Fair and Frankfurt Book Fair. A conservatory drop-out composer and musician, he read Philosophy at University of London with a critical thesis on post-truth value and normativity.

His main philosophical work lies at the intersection of ethics and aesthetics, with academic interests including social sciences, intellectual history, management and philology.

In 2022, *"Love Don't Pay the Bills"* marked his return to publishing verse, immediately followed by the other retrieved chapbooks from his Youth Poems trilogy: *"Comfortable in the Chaos"* and *"The Joy of Missing Out"*.

Hilarious and heartfelt as a Pixar character, Bozzino speaks four languages and actively combines creative writing with music, on the back of a career in business management and high finance.

www.ingramcontent.com/pod-product-compliance
Lightning Source LLC
Chambersburg PA
CBHW042320090526
44585CB00024BA/2663